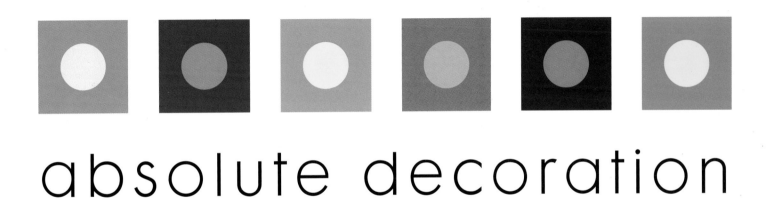

absolute decoration

Author

Arco Architects & Publishers Studio

Publishing director

Nacho Asensio

Texts

George W. O'Sullivan / Ingrid Bosch / Sharon Cagney

Esther de Puig / Andrés Llovera / Laura Fortuny

Collaborations

Elena Calderón /"Marie Claire"/ Rubén Gómez

Cristina Rodriguez

Photography

David Cardelús

Graphic design & Layout

David Maynar

Copyright © 2000 Francisco Asensio Cerver
Published by Atrium International
Ganduxer, 115, 4ª
08022 Barcelona. Spain
Phone: +34–93 418 49 10 Fax: +34–93 211 81 39
E-mail: arcoedit@idgrup.ibernet.com
Dep. Leg.: B-48560-99
ISBN: 84-8185-224-4
Printed in Spain for: SA de Litografía
Ramón Casas, 2. 08911 Badalona
Preprint: Litografía Preimpresión SA
Torrent de Vallmajor, 26. 08911 Badalona

Contents 4

Introduction

Today, more than ever, the stresses and strains of everyday life have lead us to turn our homes into oasis of tranquillity, where we can disconnect and unwind. Achieving such an atmosphere involves more than just having the right distribution of spaces. The rooms must contain elements to give them personality, to make them attractive. In short, the rooms of a house should be decorated with objects that reflect their dwellers´ personalities. The decoration of a house is vital if its residents are to feel at ease within their environment. An architectural master piece loses all its charm when badly decorated. A discrete dwelling with the right kind of decoration, on the other hand, can be very attractive and comfortable to live in.

The aim of this volume is offer a broad overview of the art of decorating. The reader will discover a wide range of elements and ideas and, above all, will learn about the art of choosing, combining and adopting these elements. We have left the theory aside to concentrate instead on specific types and styles used in various countries around the world.

Most of these spaces have been created by renowned professionals (some of the rooms reproduced within this book belong to the designers themselves) and also by people with ideas and unique decorative tastes. We have tried to cover a little of every thing, from the latest designs of lofts to country houses, and from design furniture to the simplest items.

This work provides numerous ideas that readers can use or adapt to their homes without having to spend a large sum of money. Among the many subjects included are:

- Colors of walls, fabrics, wood, and furniture.

- Period bathtubs, taps, WCs and materials.

- Flavor and color in kitchens, with solutions for storing food and crockery.

- All manner of styles and types of tiles.

- Fabrics and upholsteries, textures and various colors.

- Translucent, bevelled glass, etc.

- A wide range of lighting, from glass tear-shaped lamps to simple design light bulbs.

- Wooden illumination sculptures and ephemeral floral montages.

- Solutions for open double spaces and split levels.

- Computers, bicycles, household appliances, etc., brimming with functionality and aesthetics.

- Solutions for dealing with awkward spaces.

This short list is merely an example of the usefulness of this tome and the help it can provide readers with when they come to decorate their homes.

I believe that everyone will find something in this book, even if it is a piece of furniture, a plastic cup, a simple detail or a flower whose color matches the tone of a specific wall, which will help to make their dwelling a more comfortable place to live in.

Technology, elegance and modernity

Today´s lifestyle has forced us to undergo radical changes in comparison with how we lived only a few years ago, not only in terms of aesthetics but also in practicality. The reasons are numerous and very varied. Among the most important are the difficulty in finding a place in the city center and the exorbitant price we have to pay per square meter. This has forced many young people out into the suburbs, rehabilitating former semi-industrial zones as industries have moved away from big cities.

Having had to adapt to a style of decoration and distribution imposed by factories, a new concept of dwelling has arisen. Now the favored type of housing consists of large open spaces, in which all everyday domestic activities are carried out. In other words, everything takes place within the four main walls of the space: cooking, reading, sleeping, eating, etc. Even the bathroom is sometimes partially integrated, the WC being the only space to be fully closed off.

This way of designing a home has come about due to changes in certain types of lifestyle and, as a consequence, has compelled manufacturers of furniture, household and lighting appliances to radically reevaluate their products. Thus, pieces of furniture must now be light, neutral and as versatile as possible, since they will have to cohabit with all manner of styles and utilities. For example, in this type of loft -the name given to housing in industrial premises- the bookcase is often very large and is used to store everything in the house. Books, cutlery, objects, bottles, the television and music system, files, etc., are all kept in a single piece of furniture.

It is also important to bear in mind that household appliances must be aesthetic, since they will be permanently "on display" and it is also indispensable that they are technically well-thought out and practical. So, for example, extractor fans need to be powerful, since the cooking is virtually done in the living room, and the refrigerator and the washing machine should not be noisy. This type of home has given rise to a new range of domestic appliances that were previously not considered indispensable such as clothes dryers, which are now essential because there is nowhere to hang clothes inside a loft.

Materials have also been affected by this change, the fashion now being dyed or painted cemented paving, or parquet, which is also installed even in areas of water. Paints have made giant strides in terms of quality and resistance, and the reason for this is the same: kitchens or bathrooms within full view cannot be tiled in the old style of bathroom. They must be designed in a way that the main zones are coordinated with the other areas, and they must be decorated with a durable paint.

The first part of this chapter examines the latest decorative tendencies and the way in which old apartment houses have been renovated in order to obtain a more up-to-date appearance and achieve a dwelling that is able to cope with the requirements of today´s lifestyle. This all boils down to a double objective: a house that is comfortable to reside in and suitable for carrying out everyday activities and, furthermore, a place that, thanks to its attractive decoration, is an oasis of relaxation and tranquility, within a world in which noise, time and stress never cease to harass us.

Boldness, Color, Recycling and design

Imagination is one the most essential factors for decorating with color, recycling anything we have around us, and redistributing space in order to achieve a new look with the same elements used in the previous decoration. The difficult part is knowing how to begin, but once your imagination is let loose, it is capable of working miracles. It is surprising how inventive one can be when learning how to look at objects under a new prism. Therefore in this section in particular and in the book as a whole, you will find a multitude of atmospheres, details, ingenious innovative and attractive ideas that can be used to initiate admirers of decoration in this new field of decoration, based on creativity, color application and the recycling of objects.

Learning how to rid ourselves of conventions and see our home as a space in we can experiment takes a little bit of getting used to. Changes and innovations do tend to scare us. Anything daring, a departure from the norm, is, in reality, a step into unknown territory, the result of which invariably produces a feeling of satisfaction.

The importance and the advantages of recycling and using color in decoration are many. With the millennium coming to a close, everyone is now conscious of the need to not waste or squander anything. Recycling is the order of the day.

Furthermore, nowadays, furniture and decorative objects are highly priced, and we are not always able to afford a complete change in decoration, neither are we ready to buy everything new when we change apartments nor purchase a piece of dream furniture when it is not really necessary. Recycling is cheap and fun and, without doubt, it gives a house a completely personal touch. Because there is one thing we can be absolutely sure of: if you find an alternative use for a piece of furniture, paint it in a special color and give it a different finish to wood, you won´t find anything like it anywhere in the world: it is unique.

The examples reproduced in this section will inevitably lead to so many other ideas and suggestions that it immediately becomes clear how infinite the options are and, regardless of how difficult it a room may appear, there will always be a something that at first sight seemed condemned to failure can be turned into an interesting and attractive result with personality.

Countryside, seaside, harmony and light

The aim of decorating a second home is not so much for mere elegance as for the necessary comfort that will allow its inhabitants to disconnect and unwind from the problems of everyday life. In other words, they must are able to "feel at home". Just as with everything else, it is indispensable to pay attention to the most suitable forms to obtain the right color and tonal balance in shape and rhythm. The size and structure of the space -as well as the quality of the walls and floor- the volumes, the colors, and illumination are all essential factors for achieving such a balance and harmony. How adequate or not these factors are depends on the sensation perceived: comfort, elegance, informality, saturation or incoherence.

Daylight is a fundamental element in country houses, not only because it dictates the distribution of spaces but because the sources of natural light - apertures, doors, skylights, glass windows - are, together with porches and conservatories, the connection between the interior and the exterior, the transition between the protected interior and the elements. The architecture of a dwelling apt for the lighting conditions vary in accordance with the climatological characteristics and the idiosyncrasies of each geographical location.

It is not essential that a country house be of a rustic design. One of the most pleasant styles of decoration is that inherited from the great rural mansions, in which we find excellent combinations between the popular and the sumptuous that are the reflection of different cultures, and which give way to combinations of exceptional personality and unique attractiveness. The English cottage, a traditional 19th century second residence, provides an excellent example along these lines. The cottage is a realm of detail: fabrics, light fittings, flower vases, etc. Soft pastel tones, in accord to local taste, can be contrasted with wood and a few porcelain items.

There is a wide variety of highly attractive styles to choose from in order to lend elegance to a country house, but there is one rule to always bear in mind: a country home´s greatest asset is its space. Therefore it is indispensable to avoid cluttering the space with furniture and complements. You should know the number of items required and, above all, their quality. It is always better to use few objects, although they must have the necessary character and personality. Avoid mediocrity at all costs. The intrinsic quality of the elements is fundamental, and is responsible, to a large degree, to the increased popularity of antiques.

Another popular place for second homes is by the sea. Given our habits, costal dwellings often have a beach personality. Whereas the rusticity of the traditional country house is solid and cozy, the house by the sea breathes vitality, luminosity, a cheerful environment decorated with dynamic colors. The most popular forms of decorating often include tiles, furniture made of wicker or varnished wood, brass light fixture, brightly-colored ceramics, and so on. This type of house is more often than not used on a seasonal basis, and as such it is important to bear in mind one practical factor when choosing the decoration: make it easy to keep clean. Regardless of the case, you will always have to work over a structure whose construction elements remain visible, close to nature and with spaces that cry out for attractive details.

This chapter offers a variety of ideas for decorating a second residence. The ideas and photographs included within this section will show you how to put into practice everything that has been mentioned above.

Taste, bathrooms and accesories

The rustic kitchen is based on several inevitable elements and materials: wood, china, glistening copper pots, terrazzo floors and solid, sturdy furniture. Although this style of decor gives the impression that it is made to last several generations, it has managed to adapt itself so that it still fits in nicely with the latest appliances that are part of the practical, modern kitchen. In fact, the contrast between the new materials and ergonomic design and the typically rustic components provides endless decorative possibilities for both the kitchen and bathroom. This has resulted in the rediscovery of many traditional components which had long been forgotten, such as the classic cast-iron stoves from the first half of this century. Of course, underneath their old-fashioned surface lies the most up-to-date technology.

A similar tendency has emerged in the bathroom. The latest, most sophisticated Jacuzzis are installed next to traditional materials such as ceramic, which have evolved in unexpected ways. Over the last few decades, the bathroom has transformed itself from the basic toilet to a sophisticated area dedicated to personal hygiene. A new breed of interior decorators has cropped up, dedicating themselves to the planning and decoration of the various spaces, surfaces, contours, and materials of this once-forgotten area of the home. Aspects such as plants, textiles and finishes, which were once only given serious consideration when decorating the more "important" parts of the house, are now an important part of bathroom decor.

Rustic furniture has become so popular that it is now common to manufacture new chests, tables and sideboards in several styles, such as Provençal, Alpine, Norman or Castilian. These pieces are then treated with paint and varnish using techniques designed to give them an aged, antique appearance. There are a large number of companies which produce this type of furniture, whereas others manufacture glass, china, and ceramic accessories that reproduce traditional crafts or invent new ones in related styles. These various styles of rustic decor have become a ubiquitous presence in modern decor. Although this tendency is most often used in kitchens and dining rooms, it has spread to other parts of the house, such as the bedroom, living room, and study, with surprising success.

Two accessories in particular deserve special attention: carpets and fireplaces. These elements often form the central motifs of a decorative scheme, albeit in different ways. The fireplace is an obvious center of attention, since it invites the members of the household to gather around the warmth and light it provides. For this reason, the rest of the decor should normally be organized around the fireplace. A rug, on the other hand, is a more discrete accessory which can nevertheless enhance a well-decorated room. Some carpets, however, are works of art in their own right which can fill an entire room with their presence. Wood, ceramics, a glowing fireplace, and a beautifully woven rug are enough in themselves to create a warm and inviting atmosphere.

This section brings together several suggestions and ideas which we hope will provide a range of solutions to various problems in home decoration.

Doubles spaces, vestibules and organization

Lofts currently very fashionable. The trend of turning them into dwellings allows us to take maximum advantage of the square meters available by creating mezzanines and split-level residences, in which some of the rooms have views to others. Furthermore, the need to take advantage of the space has compelled interior decorators and architects to find a way to get the most out of what was previously considered as transit zones, such as entrance halls and vestibules.

Hallways, passageways and vestibules are the most common areas of transit in virtually all dwellings. Each one of these areas has its own identity, for which reason we will examine them individually. Nonetheless, they do share certain aspects that require similar treatment. For instance, since they are used for going from one room to another, their walls and floors require resistent materials; they must be unobstructed and have practical, low-consumption illumination.

As a rule, entrance halls are small and have scarce illumination. This is not a problem since any activity here does not usually last very long.

If the entrance hall connects to an exterior room that has light, it is indispensable to take advantage of it, either by removing the door connecting the two spaces and replacing it with a partition that allows light to pass through, or a door made of glass.

Regarding artificial illumination, a discrete light is all that is required. The best way to gain space is by using spotlights fitted into the ceiling, although wall lamps or, depending on the choice of decoration, a small table lamp are equally appropriate.

The decoration of the entrance is especially important because it is the first impression the visitor has on entering the house. One of the first things to bear in mind when decorating an entrance hall are its dimensions. If it is a very small space, you can hang a mirror, which visually increases the size of the room, complementing it with a hat or coat stand and a small bench. Another option would be to leave it clear and install a discrete cupboard for hanging coats and hiding the electricity meter. With enough space, you can furnish it with everything: a coat stand, a small easy chair and a suitable table or secretaire for keeping mail, writing notes, and so on, provided they do not obstruct the way.

Since there is much coming and going through an entrance hall, it is important to decorate it in a functional manner and ensure it is uncluttered. Glass doors are ideal for these zones to allow the light to reach them from an adjoining room, if it is an exterior room. A console table or other light piece of furniture provides decoration without diminishing the space of narrow entrance halls and vestibules, while you can also place cupboards, bookcases and other items of furniture if there is enough space. One way to give warmth and elegance to this type of space is to use books or colonial furniture as a form of decoration. Rugs also play an important role, as can be observed in the photographs. Here we are mainly concerned with small rooms because they are more difficult to decorate than large ones, since the solutions must be adapted to its confines. In order to achieve this, people often resort to furniture that is made to measure, of which this section should give you an idea. Mirrors also help to make a space appear bigger than it really is if you know how to use them decoratively. Last, it is paramount to take care with details like curtains, roller blinds, paintings and ornaments. All these possibilities that can be employed in decoration are included in this chapter, with the aim of providing readers with enough examples to allow them to decorate their duplexes, entrance halls, vestibules and passageways.

Details, lighting and plants

There is nothing so pleasant as contemplating the final details to add to the decoration. As opposed to the abstractness involved in conceiving a space that is both functional and aesthetic, the detail is more concrete, easier to understand and, in many cases, fascinating. It may be a picture of some kind, a corner you want to use in a creative way, or a decorative complement to place next to your favorite item of furniture. It is important to bear in mind, nonetheless, that the impact produced by detail is such that it can distract the observer from seeing the most important aspect of a room. Likewise, it is worth remembering that decoration based exclusively on details will never be harmonic, and will rarely look pleasant no matter how aesthetic the areas may be.

Therefore it is important to first begin with the most indispensable, and work your way toward the finer details. But you must also take advantage of those pleasant moments of inspiration, ensuring they fit in with the general decorative scheme, because a single motif, or a variety of tones of a single color can be used to consolidate a specific room. In order to achieve this, it is crucial to reevaluate the room´s center of attention and detail, which will enable you to highlight the most suitable spaces by creating areas of attention and areas of visual relaxation.

By studying and planning the main focal points, or predominate, emphatic, subdominant or subordinate accents, allows an organic treatment of each area of the house, and of each room, thus permitting us to identify which details - the subordinate accents- really contribute to lending a decorative scheme personality. Every space acquires a rhythm in which its distinctive accents take part, and we have to decide which rhythm is most apt, be it the solemnity of a waltz, which follows the main beat, or a more dynamic beat like jazz, where attention is focussed on the secondary rhythms. Rhythm, therefore, provides balance, the way everything fits together to make a whole.

In this section, we will examine several concrete situations, provide practical ideas for areas and spaces that often do not receive the attention they really deserve, such as the case of entrances. In current-day building, the hallway runs the risk of becoming a dead space due to its various functions: transit, representation, a junction between various areas... One factor that is essential for all these considerations is light, direct or indirect daylight if possible, which must achieve a rhythm between the objects placed to welcome a caller (an umbrella stand, a coat rack, etc.), furnishing for keeping small objects in (a small chest of drawers for the keys, etc.) and those that define the personality of the home, such as paintings or artistic objects.

Offices, studios and work areas, spaces that are designed for one specific function, creating an atmosphere that facilitates concentration allows the work to be organized in the most effective way. The entire space has to be coordinated, even though it may have various functions: the table, the filing cabinet -an element that can easily kill any room if it is not located in the right place- shelf space, cupboards, and lamps form a whole in that they define the personality of its occupier. Even the telephone can help to lend that which, in this case, could be considered a corporative image. These are areas that tend to be decorated little by little, with various personal objects, a factor that must be taken into account when planning them, thus avoiding cluttered spaces.

Mezzanines can equally be as functional, elastic and pleasant places as the studios. A tall ceiling can be a godsend if you know how to use it in order to create useful spaces and achieve a dynamic effect of plasticity with a split-level design, in the living room, for instance, or in the bedroom. Mezzanines provide us with a source of useful and fun ideas.

Lighting is the most important and the cheapest of all the elements that go into designing a home. Although daylight is indispensable, artificial lighting can surpass it with the latest technology available in lighting and design. There are several forms of lighting to choose from: general lighting, which is used to substitute daylight; atmospheric light, which creates an atmospheric effect by means of lamps and spotlights situated in the lower half of the room, playing with the effects of half light; complementary and work lighting, which can bring a corner - a detail- to life; special forms of lighting, such as candles, which create a, intimate and subdued atmosphere around them. In decoration we should regard light as the air supply of the elements situated within a dwelling. Without it, the furniture and ornaments could not exist. So the choice of position and style of lamps is something that should never be left to the last minute, because it requires planning, such as installing an appropriate electrical installation, with the right plugs and sockets.

Technology, elegance and modernity

Today´s lifestyle has forced us to undergo radical changes in comparison with how we lived only a few years ago, not only in terms of aesthetics but also in practicality. The reasons are numerous and very varied. Among the most important are the difficulty in finding a place in the city center and the exorbitant price we have to pay per square meter.

High technology in the home

We have already discussed that when speaking of the distribution of space within the home, the decorative style high-tech appears, not only as a collection of decorative possibilities, but also as a response to current needs that derive from today's lifestyle and the pressing lack of space from which virtually all homes suffer. The most blatant example of this problem is the ongoing conversion of old warehouses and workshops into livable homes which, without losing a smidgen of their original personality and industrial tour de force, create spaces that are generously proportioned and offer a full spectrum of possibilities.

These result in ingenious and singularly attractive homes that provide full comfort while adapting themselves perfectly to whatever function desired. This type of building is most appropriate for high-tech decoration because the metal structure, the brick walls, and the original beams and columns adapt themselves perfectly to a style that seeks comfort, aesthetics and function through a cold and austere uniformity. The frequent use of industrial furniture and objects combine with the ultimate in high technology appliances.

Nonetheless, in spite of what we have just noted, this style is not exclusive to industrial spaces. Any city apartment can serve to evoke at least the spirit of this style, given that many of the elements particular to high-tech, such as metallic spotlights, aluminum floor tiles or metal supermarket shelves, can be combined with highly attractive results in any living space.

Here below we point out a list of guidelines regarding the types of furniture and complementary items that can help us develop this handsome and loose, cheerful and informal environment, and the relaxing and peaceful atmosphere that homes decorated in this style possess.

• The area, whether large or small, must be as open as possible, eliminating partitions and separations. Living room, kitchen and dining room all share the same space and so all the furniture and the rest of the materials must be a collection that is aesthetically harmonious, even though they will be distributed throughout differentiated zones or separate environments within the home.

• Given that the design must evoke the clear and evident sensation of a small industrial or workshop environment, it is crucial to avoid a mish-mash of styles. Therefore, the furniture and their complements must be few and functional, and not overloaded. They must have an industrial aspect; beds with pieces of scaffolding, metal shelves and stairs, brass laminates, a large ventilator on the ceiling.

• The walls, following the formula of the decoration, should maintain their old, warehouse appearance (although cleaned up) whenever possible, given that this is in keeping with the original atmosphere of the space. If this isn't viable, the walls can be finished with uncovered brickwork, glass tiles, or aluminum panels.

• The forms of the decorative elements (tables, chairs, shelving, windows) must be in general geometrically well defined, utilizing mostly squares and rectangles.

• The most advanced technology with respect to both air conditioning and heating units and audiovisual and electrical kitchen appliances, are well adapted to this industrial image. They additionally lend a modern air to the home and minimize the disadvantages of living in this sort of architectural space.

• The lighting can be minimal, but must always be functional, with frequent use of spotlights or industrial-grade florescent

Creating a double-use piece of furniture is a way of generating space in the bedroom, for example, a closet that doubles as a headboard on the back side. This solution provides a sort of dressing room /corridor area behind the bed.

bulbs. Natural light through wide and large windows should in any event be taken advantage of at every opportunity in this style.

• The most appropriate window shading would be metallic Persian blinds, or the windows can even be left uncovered.

• The design of the staircase becomes especially important for the overall effect of the space, and should be free of handrails. There should be scant furniture and of a technological design. If the house is one open space but requires divisions, these can be made of frosted glass for walls and doors to maintain a sense of privacy. In this way, the sensation of a large space that the environment offers is not broken.

• It is a good idea to include some decorative pieces, particularly porcelain or glass objects with geometrical shapes. This type of decoration is quite original and has a special attractive quality, but it can seem cold and a bit sterile. Ornamental pieces can without a doubt infuse the collection with a certain dynamism and youth.

One of the most striking characteristics of high-tech decorative criteria is its sobriety. It never includes superfluous ornamentation, eliminating any non-functional decorative elements. The concept of space is the most important aspect.

In modern, avant-garde decoration, the tendency is not to disguise elements but to make them more evident. Therefore, this kitchen is integrated right into the most noble area of the home, with no dividing elements.

Industrial living spaces

Until recently, a house was conceived as a building designed to be inhabited by people who carry out their daily life there, and was associated with an almost invariable structure and distribution. Although the decoration, arrangement and style might vary, houses have always conformed to certain fixed, universal underlying concepts.

About twenty years ago, cities began to suffer an increasing lack of living space, and it became necessary to find new kinds of housing that corresponded to new lifestyles. In an effort to meet this need, interior decorators developed a new style: the revolutionary concept of high-tech design. This tendency often involves redecorating, or even transforming, buildings that were not originally designed as houses or apartments, such as factories, warehouses or workshops.

The tendency when working with this type of spaces is to preserve the original structure, with its beams and pillars, as much as possible while creating a space within it. Sheer volume, rather than decoration or architecture, is highlighted, and full advantage is taken of the high ceilings, the characteristically industrial design, and the great quantity of light that streams in through the large original windows, filling every corner of the space.

The resulting large, open spaces, as well as the cold, geometric atmosphere characteristic of this kind of design, lend themselves to the concept of the house as one unified open space with no barrier between the different areas or 'rooms'. Walls, doors and other separating devices are eschewed in favor of one integrated space for cooking, eating, reading, or entertaining guests. The result is a multi-purpose room divided into different areas according to use, but the whole remains unified and with a clearly defined personality. The noises and interferen-

ce that might normally be expected in this kind of arrangement are not a problem in this kind of house because of the ample space and high ceilings.

The high ceilings in this type of building allow not only for the construction of lofts but also of a mezzanine within the same structure. This is common practice in this kind of building, since it fits in well with the austere aesthetics of industrial design. In order to accentuate the structure's unique personality, the staircase that connects the two levels should be left in plain view and conserve its original material (aluminum or steel), as well as the sharply defined geometric shapes typical of old industrial warehouses.

A great deal of the originality of this style of decoration proceeds from the surprisingly effective use of buildings that were originally constructed for work. For this reason, the dominant motif should emphasize shades of gray, industrial materials, and the square and rectangular shapes frequently used in offices.

The walls, floors and furniture, combined and connected to each other, should form a unified whole in order to create a coherent atmosphere that enhances its spaciousness. This style of decoration gives an impression of youth, novelty and uniqueness, and its attraction lies in the spurning of conventions and stereotypes. These buildings, perhaps more than any others, provide a wealth of possibilities for the expression of personal taste and character.

Nevertheless, the difficulty inherent in high-tech design arises from its characteristic simplicity and functionality. The number of pieces of furniture and other decorative objects should be kept to a minimum in keeping with the cold, spare architectural style. Similarly, there is no place for whims when choosing the

The staircase is the decorative center of attention in this home.
Its svelte and light ascent and its simple lines lend
a dominate note to this high-tech interior design that was conceived to rehabilitate
this space, where it was well worth installing a mezzanine.

The L shape of this interior and the location of the windows add enormously to the success of the decoration in this open space in which each element has its place.

finishes and accessories. The shades of colors should also be adapted to this style, with a predominance of whites and grays, although an occasional point of contrast in black or other basic colors can also produce an interesting effect.

This bathroom consists of two separate areas. The bathtub and toilet are in the bathroom proper, while the sink and counter space are located just outside in the dressing room. Both areas combine to form the bathroom space.

This bathroom was created out of an unused corner at the end of a hallway. It has been designed in the simplest possible way, playing with the different floor levels and preexisting materials of the original area, combining them to enhance the decorative effect.

Decorating the first home

A home is something more than a house. It is where an important part of life takes place and where the personal objects most identified with an individual are kept, where the daily activities of a family occur or where the most intimate time alone is spent. This is where the most personal of stamps is placed. The home in a certain sense synthesizes an important part of life and defines the character and the personality of those who live there.

When the time comes to decorate a first home, a number of doubts can develop that might seem impossible to resolve. A couple can lose sleep trying to determine which is the appropriate sofa for the new living room, how to outfit the bedroom for the children that they want to have, which elements and what range of colors will be best for the kitchen or bathroom, or whether it is necessary, or even possible, to carry out certain reforms to give the house a different and improved appearance.

Decorating is not easy. Nonetheless, success is not something to be afraid of. Decorating can be like a fun game with no fixed rules, where intuition, dreams and good taste are enough to change the first home into the dream house. Furnishing a house means formulating and carrying out particular ideas for the entire living space, converting the home into something personal and filled with character. The successful decoration of a home must reflect the life of those who live there and support and express their manner of living, their likes, needs and preferences.

A house should be selected with an eye to ensuring it receives proper natural light, that it is in good condition, and that everything functions properly. After this selection, the best plan is to keep calm and avoid making rash decisions, taking time to decide how the house should really be decorated. It is counterproductive to try to have everything in place before moving in.

Otherwise, when the home is found to have certain uncomfortable attributes, or it doesn't have the desired aesthetic qualities,

it will be more difficult tomake the necessary changes in the distribution.When entering into a home for the first time the inhabitant frequently possesses little or no furniture. In this case, the often-limited available funds should be spent on the most important and basic elements: tables and comfortable chairs for the dining room, a good bed, and a nice sofa. The details and complements must be taken care of bit by bit. Reflection and daily experience will clarify many doubts and will help to resolve each problem as it arises.

The living room/dining room is one of the most important areas in the house, since this is where most of the family life takes place. It is the place where guests are entertained and where a lot of resting and relaxing takes place. It is highly recommended at the outset to furnish the dining room with a lamp, a table and chairs. The living room should include at a minimum a sofa, a center table and a standing lamp. These items are clearly just the bare essentials. Later, living in the home will help to determine real necessities, both those that are practical and functional as well as those that are aesthetic.

The rooms seen here are separated simply by a change of floor tiles to differentiate the spaces instead of resorting to the traditional door.The rest can be decorated gradually according to personal taste, substituting the initial furnishings and adding others.

The bathroom and kitchen are probably the rooms that can best be decorated before moving in. This is because there are certain basic fixtures and appliances which are necessary to these rooms and whose use and function are obvious. The task

The steps of the central stair also function as a small display area.

here is to select the decorative line that is best adapted to the dimensions of the spaces and the decorative whole of the home. It is important to remember that appliance fixture models that are to be installed before moving into the house should be chosen carefully. They should be able to adapt themselves perfectly to the dimensions of the space and allow for the comfortable movement of the inhabitants. Their distribution should also be logical and appropriate for the function that they are to perform.

The bedroom is also an important area for it can't be denied that the manner and surroundings in which one awakes affects the rest of the day. Decorating a bedroom does not mean simply filling it with objects. It is therefore best to lean towards the simplicity and comfort of a good bed, a pair of nightstands with reading lamps and a practical closet. Just as in other rooms, it is of primary importance to procure a few well-chosen elements that reflect the personality of the inhabitant. Time spent in the home will determine later which details are most necessary and important.

In this open space, cladding colours and murals are used to delineate the different areas.

The warmth of bare brick visually dominates this interior.

A collection of modern artsworks is arranged around an unusual glass and iron credenza.

Different areas are marked out with a series of rugs.

Modifications in the house

When moving into a new home, we find it is often already conveniently finished and ready to live in comfortably at the outset. Nonetheless, because of particular needs or uses, or because of changes in the number of family members, it will sometimes be necessary to carry out some remodeling or refurbishing. This constitutes an important topic that must be thoroughly taken into consideration before beginning to work.

Various circumstances may call for remodeling the home. A change in the number of family members, the need for new space for use as a workplace, children who previously shared a room who have become older and as a result need separate bedrooms, or simply the desire to create more lighting and ventilation in some space that has no window or just a small one. Any of these circumstances may require structural modifications to make the space suitable for the needs that the new circumstances warrant.

At times, particularly when spaces must be divided or separated, whether for economic reasons or for the mere fact that the desired results can be attained without undue cost outlays, one can resort to certain decorative solutions, such as different flooring levels, different color tones in the two spaces or folding screens or dividing furniture. But when the project involves the physical enlargement of a space, the opening of a window or door, or the annexation of a new space to the principal house, it will be necessary to make some type of alteration to the architectural structure.

Before making any decision, the first thing to do is think carefully about the changes that are desired. If the steps to be taken to guarantee the outcome are not absolutely certain, the best option would be to resort to professional help. It is not advisable to start on this type of work without a working knowledge of what is to be done. A million problems can arise with plumbing, rerouting electric cables or other unpleasant surprises that often occur as construction work is performed. It must not be forgotten that certain reforms affecting the external part of a living space (such as opening a door or window) often require legal permits, which assure that the work in progress will not harm the neighbors nor break the aesthetics unity of a building.

Before starting a project of any size or complexity, it is important to take into consideration how long you intend to live there, or whether the home is rented or owned. These sorts of modifications require a considerable investment of time and money, and, after thinking about it, perhaps the conclusion should be drawn that another solution is more appropriate.

Internal reforms are the most frequent, specifically the enlargement of a room, the division of a room into two rooms, or the opening up of interior windows and doors to facilitate the passage to and from distinct spaces. There are various advantages of transforming two small rooms into one larger room. Two children can share the same bedroom, a comfortable bedroom/walk-in closet can be created from two small, uncomfortable rooms that had no room for closet space, or a bathroom can be enlarged.

If the wall to be knocked down is a supporting wall, it will be necessary to call in an expert, since some method of supporting the weight that was on the wall will have to be created. If it is not a supporting wall, taking it out causes no real problems, but it is helpful in any event to think about the aesthetic and practical results desired before removing it. If, for example, you want to connect the kitchen with the dining room, the best solution might not be to completely eliminate the separating wall, but instead create a wide opening in the form of an arch. This would

The living room and bedroom have a common denominator in the flooring. Following the modern concept of interior design, this bedroom is laid out so that the bed, dressing room and bathroom form an integrated unit.

The decoration of this corner is quite emphatic in that everything revolves around one repeated geometrical shape. The focus is on the cube in three-dimensional objects, the square on flat surfaces. This repetition provides the space with coherence.

Porch with a high shelf to take advantage of space and create a cozy corner.

serve the functional and attractive purpose of dividing the different environments within the same space. The same is true if more than one activity is intended in the new space. The intimacy is maintained while smaller, more claustrophobic spaces are avoided. An intermediate solution is to install some sliding doors that can allow the entire room to be used without eliminating the ability to occasionally separate the room into two distinct spaces as the need arises.

Sometimes joining two spaces into one creates a space with an irregular form. In this case the irregularities can be taken advantage of to establish small sub-spaces for various activities. It isn't absolutely necessary to make the flooring uniform throughout the annexed spaces, especially since this could mean a big cost outlay. Nonetheless, single flooring for the new space is an efficient way of visually unifying what was before two separate spaces.

Something important to keep in mind is that it is not easy to imagine what the rooms will be like before they are built. It wouldn't be the first time that the results of constructing a partition definitively establish that the two newly created rooms are too small and cramped for their intended use, that the cure is found to be worse than the disease. One practical solution is to examine a room that has similar dimensions to that which is to be created, to assure that it will serve its intended purpose. If this is not feasible, make a small plan drawn to scale along with some cutouts of the furniture to be included in the space, also made to scale. The furniture cutouts can then be moved around to determine their proper distribution and whether or not the planned space is adequate for its intended use.

Porches have long been relegated to domestic uses such as washing, sewing or ironing. Today, these narrow, nearly exterior areas, in addition to the many functions they can fulfill, have come to be seen as excellent places to sit and relax, for they are cheerful, sunny and tranquil.

Living in a split-level home

When everyone today laments the lack of space in homes, to speak of a split-level (a duplex or two-story apartment), almost seems sarcastic. But there are still some split-level homes available secondhand. In some cities they might even include some form of an attic, with a large, unutilized space that can be perfectly rehabilitated as a complement to the home. With a bit of luck, this attic could substantially augment the available living space of the home.

Homes with two floors are scarcer in cities with each passing day. The enormous demand for homes, the high price of habitable square footage and the resulting high costs for their purchase has meant that split-level homes are being built with less and less frequency. To live in a split-level today is almost the exclusive domain of single family dwellings on the outskirts of an urban environment. Nevertheless, two floors can offer excellent possibilities and host a series of comforts that, with the hustle and bustle of city life, perhaps have been forgotten or at least underestimated. The advantages are such that if economic conditions so allow, it is actually advisable to add to a floor by annexing the apartment directly above. To be sure, the results will be more than satisfactory.

A home with two floors does admittedly bring into the equation a certain displacement among the rooms and some resultant inconveniences, since certain spaces will be far from others. Because of this fact, the first, most important and decisive matter to address regarding a split-level home is to determine at the outset the functions that each room shall possess, so that the house will be as comfortable and as functional as possible. It is only logical that with any two-floor home a significant amount of attention should be paid to the organization of the rooms, so that there are no real problems or inconveniences resulting from poor communication between them. If, for example, the kitchen is on one floor and the dining room on another, meals will become a veritable nightmare for whoever has to go up and down the stairs to set the table, deliver the food and clean the table afterwards. If the bathroom is on a different floor from the bedrooms the inhabitants will be hugely inconvenienced every morning, when the bathrooms are most in use.

Actually, the bathroom is one of the most controversial points in the organization of a split-level home. The most recommended organization to assure maximum comfort and least complication in passage is to install a bathroom or at least a half-bathroom on each one of the floors.

If the two floors have approximately the same dimensions, the most appropriate distribution is normally to have the entranceway, living room/dining room, a bathroom and the kitchen on the ground floor. The various bedrooms, one or one and a half bathrooms, and if possible a quiet study or workroom are all located on the upper floor.

At times, one of the two floors is smaller than the other. In this case, it is normal to place a bedroom, living room or study along with a bathroom on the smaller floor, leaving the rest of the house for the larger floor.

The most characteristic element of a split-level home is the stairway. It is clear that its presence is essential, but its aesthetic and functional possibilities should be taken advantage of. If the total square footage of the home is limited, one option for capitalizing on the available space is to install a spiral staircase, preferably next to a wall, since it will always occupy less space than a more traditional staircase. If a normal staircase is nonetheless installed, the small space found underneath should not

By raising the ceiling, sufficient space has been gained in this home to add a second floor and convert it into a split-level, with the bedrooms on the upper floor and the living, dining and kitchen areas downstairs.

In this split-level, an ingenious solution has been provided for the chimney. It has been placed in the space under the staircase. For this reason, the staircase has been placed in the center of the room with a free-standing wall built in to shield it from the living room.

be ignored. It can be used for a variety of purposes: placement of a small office or desk, placement of a small telephone table, installation of a small living area, installation of closet space, use as a decorative alcove.

As a final matter, one interesting advantage that a split-level home offers is that it possesses two clearly differentiated environments which can be decorated in distinct styles or images without negative repercussions on the home's coherence. This should not, however, be used as an excuse for drastic or aggressive differences. It is always advisable to have a decorative scheme that lends a certain unity to the whole, whether it is the same flooring material or the use of a harmonious range of colors for the walls and elements in the home.

One of the simplest yet most spectacular choice of bathtubs, requiring no construction work for its installation, is the ancient one with legs instead of having a modern one built in.

The kitchen occupies an entire wall. It is laid out linearly along one edge of the living room. The decoration of both spaces is harmonious, lending continuity to colors and materials. To zone off the kitchen, some column-like parts of wall have been left behind.

Technological simplicity and comfort

After centuries of cooking and doing household chores in more or less the same way, that is, with a lot of hard work, few facilities and a considerable dedication of time, the appearance on the market of the first electric appliances and their rapid assimilation into society represented a radical change of habits, a veritable revolution in domestic lifestyles. Suddenly, an important amount of time that had been dedicated to washing clothes and dishes by hand and preparing meals was considerably reduced. This time could then be used for hobbies, studies, work or any other activity.

In time, the sophistication of these machines reached unhoped-for new levels, offering the user not only comfort and a better quality of life, but also improved hygiene, safety and efficiency in housework. As an improvement on the invention of simple automatic controls, which let you program the times when appliances will turn on and off, the latest domestic appliances are now equipped with Fuzzy Control, an electronic regulation system that permits energy savings. A washing machine with a fuzzy system has the capacity to measure out the proper quantity of detergent and water and allot the correct amount of time necessary to wash the clothes according to the weight and characteristics of the clothes to be washed. Ovens automatically control the cooking temperature appropriate for the type of food being cooked.

Ovens. The kitchen has witnessed a constant evolution in technology and design with respect to comfort, hygiene, time, etc. The traditional type, comprising an oven with a four-burner stove all in white, is becoming antiquated, and today it can be said with certainty that in the not-too-distant-future this type of oven will be considered an authentic museum piece. Today, models are made of all types of materials and come in all sizes and colors. They can be adapted to any conceivable space and style of decoration. Glazed ceramic cooking tops have replaced the old burners and can be aligned perfectly flush with the countertops. They are also much easier to clean. Some models come equipped with an electronic recognition system for pots and frying pans. The burners are only activated when objects of a certain weight are placed on them. They won't activate if they sense only small objects which may have been forgotten on them.

Magnetic induction ovens are decorative and seem more like flagstones. They don't heat up since they use magnetic energy to cook food instead of electrical heat coils or gas.

Other types of ovens come equipped with all sorts of accessories for food preparation: deep-fryers, grills, griddles, roasting spits and a combination of electric and gas burners.

There are in truth many ovens to choose from. Both the more conventional ones which emit heat and the newer models may come with a range of options: a temperature regulator for thawing or reheating, a programmable clock, a setting for steam cooking, a grill for all types of food and even a special cooking function for pizzas. Virtually all of these new models incorporate modern cleaning and safety systems. Special surfaces in the oven's interior which absorb grease are employed for cleaning, as are materials that can be cleaned with a small amount of detergent and very little effort. Carbonization systems can be used to eliminate cooking residues under high temperatures. Double or triple-paned glass oven doors prevent burning since they remain cool on the outside.

Convection ovens cook more rapidly and homogeneously because they incorporate a turbo fan that distributes the heat

Nowadays, kitchens are perceived as being laboratories where food is elaborated and processed. It is also true that, given the many hours that cooking takes up and the frequent lack of help, one has to find a way to make this task, in addition to being practical and hygienic, pleasant and comfortable. Therefore, good lighting and high-quality materials are always indispensable.

In this close-up we can see the lights on the lower edge of the cabinet which provide good lighting for the area between the sink and oven to facilitate food preparation.

Although traditionally, kitchens have a row of cabinets on the floor under the counter and one above it along the wall, today there is a tendency to eliminate the upper cabinets either partially or entirely.

evenly throughout the interior of the appliance. The most advanced are microwave ovens, which cook food in much less time and thaw frozen foods in just a few minutes. Although their original function was to heat and thaw, today they often come equipped with a grill, can perform several types of cooking simultaneously, and include an electronic regulating panel.

Refrigerators and freezers. The selection of the size and type of refrigerator will always depend upon the size of the family, the available space in the house, and the culinary habits of the inhabitants. If, for lack of time, the custom is to go shopping only once a week, it might be appropriate to acquire a separate freezer to preserve food longer. If this is not possible due to lack of space, a combined refrigerator-freezer model with a large freezer space can be chosen.

Some refrigerators today have hermetically sealed drawers for storing fruit and vegetables, where the temperature and humidity can be regulated.

Many also include a defrosting mechanism which makes this unpleasant task simple. Other small domestic chores now performed by refrigerators include automatic ice cube production and a permanent supply of cold drinking water.

In a very small kitchen, the decoration should be as unified as possible, avoiding the use of many materials. Here, only marble and steel have been used, even for the floor, creating an open, spotless and elegant look.

Decorative elegance

There is often a desire, even a need, to infuse the home with a personality that is almost artistic in scope, with an aesthetic interpretation that is concerned above all else with creating a strong visual impact as a whole. To contemplate a house in this style is like studying a painting or work of art. This constantly growing movement is known as the decorative style.

It is not easy to explain the specific characteristics of this concept of decoration since it is not identified with any specific motifs, objects or materials. Rather, it is an attempt to achieve a general visual effect that displays elegance, exuberance and a heightened artistic value. This can be obtained equally through modern elements or with classical objects, and adapts equally well to both modern-day apartments or antique homes.

It is a busy style, where a multitude of decorative objects blend with the furniture and highly aesthetic complements so that at times it seems that there is not a single free space in homes decorated in this manner. Walls are filled with paintings, old clocks or a collection of photographs. The floors are covered with rugs.

A pretty chair, bookshelf or some ornamental porcelain object is found in every corner, and the tables, desks, shelves and other furniture are covered with a blizzard of ornamental objects. The entire collection of elements that decorate or seem to almost inundate a home gives it a certain museum-like air.

It is certainly true that any type of decoration that is well thought out and executed can offer satisfactory results. Nonetheless, keep in mind that a decorative scheme in this style can be especially complicated, and the objective difficult to achieve. The baroque, over-stuffed and overwhelming nature of this style can have an effect that is contrary to that initially inten-

ded. Indeed, the sort of 'vacuous horror' which seems to be the basis for this type of decoration can easily be a double-edged sword. It is in any case absolutely essential to avoid confusing the exuberance, visual impact and the sublime nature of this aesthetic quality with a lack of comfort and functionality. If the environment so overloaded and pretentious that one can't move around comfortably or relax, it means that the decorator has taken a wrong turn somewhere.

It is obviously crucial to take special care that the practical aspect of the decoration does not interfere with the aesthetic. Naturally, period furniture pieces and other antiques are appropriate for a decoration that is based on visual impact. However, when the time comes to begin the task of decorating the space, it is good to disregard preconceived concepts and follow personal preferences, selecting elements of diverse origin and even style, for the very fact that the importance of this style lies in the final, overall visual effect.

One characteristic of this decorative style is the interplay between a collection of objects of all styles, which are similar only in that they are utilized as ornamentation. Another is the effort expended in decorating spaces that are normally ignored or given up as lost, always with the goal of reinforcing the visual image of the whole.

The entranceway holds special relevance in this sense, since it offers the first impression of the house. Hallway walls may be filled with paintings like a small gallery or lined with bookshelves, although sufficient space should be allowed for comfortable passage to and fro. It is also perfectly appropriate to take advantage of any small corner that offers a spot for a handsome chair, a small auxiliary table or any decorative element.

In the world of decoration, any attempt to create an atmosphere that is classical and at the same time elegant and in keeping with today's tastes, must inevitably resort to a play between different types of white for the color scheme. 'White on white' is once again the key element of the scene. Once again, regarding decoration, choosing white is always a sure bet for success. The results will always be satisfying.

The entire decoration of the house plays with the color white in the different fabrics and textures used: white lace curtains, lacquered or satin-finished wood and upholstery to match. Using different tones of white will almost certainly provide a successfully classical, elegant and yet modern result

In a design which seeks elegance and a traditional air, the kitchen must be in keeping with the rest of the house. Here, parquet is used and the dining area is furnished with period pieces. The lamps and paintings are fine enough for the living room area. This type of design is always attractive and dynamic, but requires skill and good taste. In addition, a few points should be kept in mind. Here, for example, the ventilator must be strong to remove all odor from cooking.

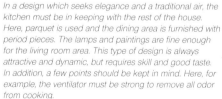

Finally, another key factor is artificial lighting. This decorative style is thought to be enhanced by this type of lighting. since its placement assists in creating the intended effect of artistic exuberance. The installation of multiple spotlights is recommended, since it helps to highlight the beauty of different pieces.

It goes without saying, although with all that has just been discussed it can surely be deduced, that a house of large dimensions is essential for this sort of decoration. In spite of the large quantity of objects and elements that are included, a generous amount of space must remain to permit freedom of movement and so avoid the sensation of an over-stuffed and claustrophobic warehouse.

To create a classical and elegant atmosphere like this one, it is essential to have the adequate space at hand. In other words, the house must be large and stately and receive a lot of light.

Classical tradition

The world of home decoration is quite varied. Individual whims and the forms of expressing them imply a virtually limitless variety of decorative techniques. Yet, while many styles have developed over the years which merit all the public attention and interest they have received from their moment of birth, it is also true that many others have proven to be little more than fleeting fashion, and are gratefully forgotten. One style of decoration which has not succumbed to this passing fancy and has endured with its essence intact is the classical style.

In the area of interior design, the classical style has never gone out of fashion. The ability of classically styled furniture from a past era to create elegant displays, and its adaptability to other styles have allowed it to remain popular. Since its inception its influence has always been found in home decoration.

As you may already know, the classical style is not really a style, but rather a series of related styles that are quite different among themselves, each with their own distinctive characteristics.

Within the classical tradition are styles that are more pompous and ornate and others that are more austere, which can include rustic furniture. Eclectic furniture is also used in an attempt to synthesize elements and characteristics of styles from different times.

In fact, the latest trends display a renewed interest in these styles, which in past eras might have overworked the pompous aspects and the overly ornate lines. Newer but still classical looks have reinvigorated this style with models that are more simple and discrete, less weighty, but certainly no less elegant and distinguished, that perfectly combine with the cheerful elements of more modern styles.

Classical decorative techniques offer fine results in many types of homes, but those that perhaps benefit most from this style and the nobility of its materials are houses with high ceilings, which more precisely evoke the type of living spaces common during the eras when this style first took root. As for furniture, the classical style need not appear outdated. Antique chairs and armchairs combine well with modern accessories of steel or acrylic, and traditional sofas and divans mix well with lacquered elements or glass surfaces.

The most characteristic pieces of classically styled furniture are large, solid wooden bookshelves, chests of drawers, small, classically designed tables, and above all else, display cabinets, elements that cannot be omitted in any space with a classical look.

Certain complements are also determining factors: Solid woods, marbles, mirrors with golden frames or fabrics with pastel tones or strong colors like blue, green or garnet, combine perfectly with this increasingly popular style.

Motifs from the classical period should also be included. The most appropriate designs represent birds, flowers, fruit and leaves or period drawings such as coats of arms or other heraldic insignia. Continuing along the same vein, stripes are preferable to squares. Lace curtains or long drapes that reach to the floor are in keeping with this style. Indeed, they are almost essential in these types of environments. Lace curtains are used in bathrooms and kitchens, but never in living rooms and dining rooms, where it is traditional to allow the lower hem of the drape to reach all the way down and touch the floor.

The drapes should always be lined, at best with some heavy material that can provide insulation, keeping heat in and muf-

Colored silk can be combined well with a period bed to create a romantic and elegant atmosphere.

The art of creation requires ceremony and ornamentation. Nothing could be more adequate than the Louis XVI
style of these chairs and mirrors, and the Baroque
upholstery. The English-style glass door with beveled and
frosted panes provides a further Baroque touch while
lightening the atmosphere somewhat.

fling outside noise, as well as protecting
the principal fabric from becoming dirty.
One elegant option that offers an attractive
aesthetic effect is to have the curtains permanently closed at the top and tied back
during the day with ribbons of fabric or
cords.

If you wish to create a classical environment, there is no need to heed the common belief that this style, and particularly
its furniture, is expensive, since it is possible today to find classical pieces that are
even less expensive than modern furniture.
The chairs might be the most expensive.
One good way of discovering pieces with
these characteristics is to frequent flea
markets. Wonderful surprises can be found
at prices that are more remarkable still.

We have already mentioned the tendency to open spaces
in lofts, split-levels and other modern homes. This example
clearly shows that removing walls and uniting diverse spaces can enhance a classical atmosphere without decrea-
sing its noble air.

This detail of the living room demonstrates that all types of styles and cultures can be
mixed as long as the furniture is of good quality and provides for an overall balanced
effect.

Boldness, Color, Recycling and design

Imagination is one the most essential factors for decorating with color, recycling anything we have around us, and redistributing space in order to achieve a new look with the same elements used in the previous decoration. The difficult part is knowing how to begin, but once your imagination is let loose, it is capable of working miracles. It is surprising how inventive one can be when learning how to look at objects under a new prism.

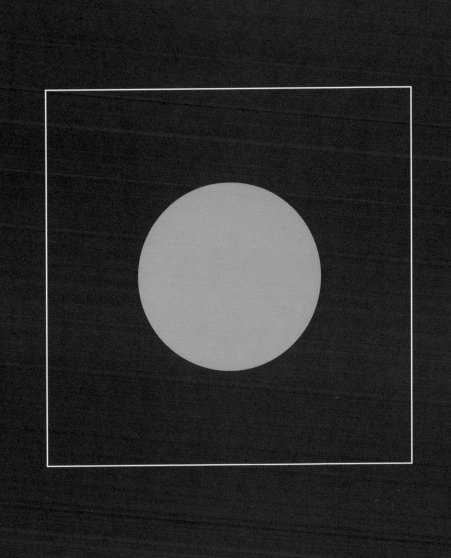

Dynamic shapes and sizes

Decorating a house involves defining a concept for its interior and making it a reality. However, a good arrangement of the available space not only gives it a personality of its own, but also brings order and practicality to daily household life. When all is said and done, the character of the house is determined by the sizes, shapes and proportions that it is composed of. This is not only true for new homes, but also for old ones that are going to be remodeled.

The spatial characteristics of any living space inevitably affect its capacities and functions (distribution of activities, circulation around the house, and ease of movement between rooms with related uses), as well as its 'look'(perspectives and lighting). For this reason it is essential to understand the dynamic possibilities that result from the various combinations of shapes and sizes.

For our purposes, a shape is any three-dimensional object that takes up some of the available space and therefore modifies and defines it. For this reason, a certain familiarity with the different kinds of shapes and the ways they can be arranged is invaluable in order to get the most out of any room. It is also useful in arranging furniture to produce different combinations that bring dynamism to a room.

The channels for circulating around the house are always the first consideration when arranging shapes. No piece of furniture should obstruct the passage from one room to another or making moving around the room difficult. The lack of space in a room can usually be disguised by an imaginative arrangement that makes the most of the available space. Some examples are: distributing the room differently, choosing dynamically designed furniture that fulfills its function without taking up too much space, and using multi-purpose or collapsible furniture.

There are three basic shapes:

Rectilinear. These are always the most abundant in any house. They appear not only in the general structures of the building (the building itself, the rooms, the hallways) but also in the furniture (tables, cabinets, beds, sofas) and complements (end tables, magazine racks, rugs, paintings, etc). A useful distinction can be drawn between pieces where the lines or silhouette are dominant, such as tables, and those which are more solid, such as a wardrobe. The former always give the impression of taking up less space, even if the dimensions are the same.

Rectilinear shapes are extremely versatile and can be adapted to any part of a room. They are especially suited to small rooms, since they allow an efficient use of space, an attribute that comes in especially handy in today's smaller apartments. On the other hand, it can become monotonous if overused. A room decorated exclusively with square and rectangular tables cabinets, lamps and couches can produce a heavy, claustrophobic effect which lacks dynamism. For this reason, rectilinear items should be mixed with other shapes. A little bit goes a long way, however; just a few well-chosen and placed objects will break up the serious, rigid effect and give the room a completely new atmosphere and a feeling of movement.

Angular. Made up of diagonal lines and angles, these shapes give a room a much more dynamic feel. Emotionally, they evoke feelings of movement, informality, freedom, and youth. The intensity of this effect depends on the size and number of the angles. Their main disadvantage is that they become tiresome after a while and need to be changed. For this reason, they are often used in small areas.

This corner would be difficult to decorate and give atmosphere without resorting to a strong element to add character. Again, the light sculptures play an essential role.

The lamp hangs from the ceiling and all of the kitchen utensils and ingredients are open to view, lending the kitchen a visual, comfortable and practical aspect. The lack of cabinets allows the viewer to enjoy the different types of crockery on display.

Curved. These dynamic and feminine shapes lend themselves to an infinite variety of combinations, but in practice they are only suited to houses with plenty of space. They are not well suited to many of today's structures, which are primarily concerned with making the most of a limited amount of space, because they necessarily waste a great deal of it when used to their maximum effect. They are, however, very useful in smaller household objects such as cups and plates, as well as in decorative elements, such as lamps and end tables. Their effect is to break up the monotony of the rectilinear shapes and bring dynamism and verve to a room.

Although they may not be eye-catchers, circles, cones, spheres and cylinders produce a pleasant visual effect in people. For this reason, although a small modern apartment may require the use of rectilinear shapes to maximize space, curved shapes can be used in smaller decorative elements, such as table legs, the backs of chairs, vases and other accessories. Perhaps the most useful and efficient examples of this are lamps.

Light sculptures help create a luminous and mysterious atmosphere in this otherwise regular bathroom. The reflections of light make patterns on the single-color tiles.

In this photograph of the same bathroom, the light sculptures continue to govern the decoration. These are shocking for their size. As you can see, this type of daring decoration resorts to a series of completely unconventional elements, colors and criteria far from the stereotype in favor of originality and personality.

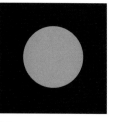

The art of reusing

Everybody, at one time or another, has found themselves with a piece of furniture or decorative element they didn't know what to do with: Old armoires that are family heirlooms but which are out of style, a chair acquired in a second-hand shop or a flea market when the economic situation didn't permit any other alternative, and which later, when substituted for a new chair, was stored away in some corner of an attic; Antique (or merely old) furniture that doesn't fit in with the decoration of the home but which is simply impossible to throw away; etc.

Many of these objects and pieces of furniture, in disuse and out of style as much for their design as for their lack of functionality, are incompatible with the practical and functional idea that governs the decoration of modern homes. Nonetheless, if given a second look, the majority of these pieces, with a bit of imagination, can be converted into a useful and even singularly decorative element.

Creating new uses for old furniture, refurbishing old chairs, lamps or tables to make them more modern, or refurbishing, polishing or waxing old desks, sideboards or consoles, is a tendency that is becoming more and more frequent in home decoration. The possibilities are endless, and many times a solution arises that is as functional as it is aesthetic. The proof is in the success of stores that sell furniture and articles made from materials and forms that attempt to imitate old secretary desks and chests. And these items are expensive, while at the same time simply do not have the same flavor and charm of an authentic, refurbished antique. They are mass-produced and usually cannot provide the personal touch of a real antique.

And so, for those old 'knickknacks' that have been absurdly stashed away in the house for years simply because no one knew what to do with them, here are some ideas for incorpora-

ting them into the decoration of the home, which can yield surprising results. But first it should be noted that it is not difficult to find, in second-hand furniture stores, antique shops, flea markets, and even at auctions, some interesting pieces at a good price that can be utilized in your home decoration.

Craft or Professional Furniture. Certain types of furniture were designed for specific professions. They were the artisans', notaries' and cabinetmakers' best allies. They had many separate compartments such as drawers, shelves, file cabinets, etc., and today are in vogue for their great versatility as well as marvelous aesthetic quality. For example, an antique herbalist's desk with its numerous small drawers can be used for a variety of things, such as classifying kitchen utensils, storing, separating and organizing garments like underclothes, handkerchiefs, socks and ties, as a sewing kit for different threads, buttons, needles and the like, as a drawer for videos, compact disks or cassettes, as a file cabinet for papers, documents, invoices, or, for the most fanatical organizer, it could serve to store all types small objects that wander loose around the house, like pens, lighters, paperclips, clothespins, etc.

It isn't really all that difficult to reuse these pieces of furniture, given that their original appearance in wood will combine with any decorative style.

Certain types of desks, bureaus and file cabinets produced for notaries and lawyers were characterized by a sliding roll-top which hid the upper desk area, along with some shelves and drawers of different sizes. These can wonderfully serve various functions while maintaining their original function as work or study desks. They can also lend a touch of classic elegance to the decoration of a space. Or, with a bit of imagination, they can be used as television, video or stereo system stands, keeping

Although any attempt at decoration should be done with a sense of measure, balance and unity, this does not mean that each room or space must be done with elements of a single style. This photograph shows the wide range of possibilities in the selection of furniture and complements in different styles but combined intelligently.

Here, a unique atmosphere of great personality has been achieved by using all the elements and furniture available, from an old basket to some sumptuous candelabra. The result is more balanced than could be expected. Candles add an excellent decorative note.

This is an atypical bedroom as it seems more like a large, eclectically furnished room presided over by a bed. Everything in it is in a different style, all the elements are different from one another. It is the daring of the concept which gives the room character.

the equipment hidden when not in use. The various drawers and shelves could even be used as a quite original shoe cabinet. If the desk does not have the roll-top it can be ideal for its attractive presence as an ornamental piece in the entrance hall or living room.

Trunks. At some point, almost everyone has found themselves with 'grandma's old trunk.' Generally speaking, no one knows what to do with it. It is bothersome as there is never a place to put it, and so at times it is thrown out. Nonetheless, these trunks can gain a special presence if, for example, they are placed as a showpiece in the entrance area. Above the trunk on the wall an elegant coat hanger or a nice painting can be hung to further show it off. A telephone, some ornamental plants or any other decorative object can be placed on top of it. If it is placed in the dining or living room, it can lend the entire room a quiet impression of sober elegance.In any case, trunks are quite useful as summertime storage for blankets and winter clothes, for which there never seems to be enough space. Or, it could be a practical place to store shoes. If the trunk is small, and the size of a bedroom not too limited, it might make just the perfect nightstand.

Seats and armchairs. Refurbishing chairs is quite simple and effective. First, sand down and varnish or paint the wood, and then upholster the seats if necessary, or change the slipcovers, using tones and patterns in accord with the rest of the decoration in the room where the chair is to be placed. The results attained will be surprising.

If the floor of the attic is weak, light furniture will have to be used. The living room area shown here is furnished with a love seat and matching armchair. A small wooden coffee table is set in the center and a chandelier with hanging glass pieces installed above it to complete the decoration.

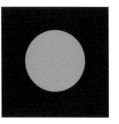

Everything in its place

For those who enjoy it, cooking can be interesting and gratifying, and has even been found to be a good remedy for stress. However, culinary work, like anything else (and possibly even more so) demands certain essential prerequisites.

To be able to perform the tasks in a kitchen with comfort and efficiency, it is indispensable that the space be pleasant, clean and orderly, that it be inviting enough for you to want to stay there for a good while amongst the pots and pans preparing a good meal. Otherwise, it becomes an unpleasant chore. It is no fun to be working in a kitchen when the sink is filled with dirty dishes, the counters are cluttered and messy and there is no adequate storage for the kitchen utensils.

The first task is to establish the proper distribution of all the elements in the kitchen space, beginning with the placement of the appliances and cabinets so as to facilitate the performance of normal kitchen activities. And so it is advisable to situate a storage area near to the entrance. This area would include a refrigerator for drinks and perishable foods, a freezer and a cupboard or closet. It is also appropriate to place shelf or counter space in this area for depositing the latest purchases before storing them.

The kitchen range is the basic component of the cooking area, which will also include a spice rack and shelving for cooking oil, salt, vinegar and other condiments used frequently when cooking, to have them within arm's reach.

The cleaning area should be situated nearby. It will consist of a one or two-basin sink. In the drawers below, the trash can is often placed, as well as the cleaning items (soap, dishwashing detergent, scouring pads, etc.). The dish rack is normally placed to the side of the sink against the wall.

Between the cooking and cleaning areas there should be a counter dedicated to food preparation. This is the area where food is cut and prepared, eggs are beaten and salads are seasoned.

Although not essential, it is quite practical to have an additional auxiliary area for storing small electrical appliances and utensils such as platters, strainers, colanders and various containers.

The perfect cupboard and cabinet space is that which can be maintained in perfect order, holding the large amount of utensils that accumulate in a kitchen, and which allows everything to be within easy arm's reach. The old concept of the pantry, which consisted of large cupboards where everything was stored together, has disappeared. In its place, cabinets and drawers are on the market that are specific to the items they are to hold and which are adaptable to any space in such a way that anything contained within is near to where it is to be used. Some are quite ingenious and original.

There are drawers of varying sizes which facilitate the classification of utensils, while taking the maximum advantage of the available space. Some are specially designed for holding pots and pans. Others incorporate a mechanism attached to the cabinet door so that when the door is opened, the shelf slides out and the provisions stored within come within easy reach, in this way avoiding the normal inconvenience of bending over and rooting around in the interior for the proper item.

A good idea to keep in mind is an auxiliary piece of furniture with wheels which, if possible folds up (carts, tables, etc.) and which can be easily moved around. This will assist in any area of the kitchen where it is needed.

This dining room is located between the kitchen and the living room. The large light-bulb has been placed as a lamp in and of itself, while the modern, extendable table is complemented by a collection of old chairs.

The headboard of this bed forms part of a wall with sliding doors providing access to the dressing room. This is a good solution for gaining space in rooms that are large enough.

Some shelves, a suitcase and an old chest, along with a simple chair, a standing lamp and a decorative bedspread are sufficient to create an aesthetic and comfortable environment in a room like this, which would otherwise be nothing particularly special.

The best way to maintain a sense of order is to create functional corners and spaces of unique atmospheres so that everything has its place and each activity is carried out in a specific area. This does not mean that there should be no double-use areas like the dining room shown here, which can be used as a study as well.

Sound planning

Changing homes or moving into an apartment for the first time is an important decision. The choice of the right home will influence your life and is not something that is simply changed or exchanged like a pair of socks. The home should express our way of being. It should synthesize and personalize our tastes, transmitting and reflecting our personality, with all of its character and feelings. Because of this, before moving into a home, and even before selecting a home, it is important to clear our minds and carefully think through what it is that we want the home to possess, what is needed to inspire us, and what is the sense that we want it to transmit.

Decorating a new home means attempting to carry out a project, or a group of personal ideas, that are representative of what we want to achieve in the space that is at our disposal. Naturally enough, the initial planning of a home will always be conditioned by the dimensions and the structure of the available space. Nevertheless, whether because of subjective perspectives or practical necessities, it is always appropriate to dedicate a considerable effort on the initial planning of the home in order to achieve the maximum results from the options that are available to us.

This will assure that our original intentions concerning the image we want the house to portray can be converted into reality. These initial, essential decisions will determine the most appropriate materials and textures for the different areas of the house, as well as the colors and elements that will be adopted in each room. The house must be a place to feel relaxed and happy. Because of this, it must be fitted to the needs of the individuals who live there. It is the center of a life, where many different activities are carried out, among which are the most fundamental aspects of a person's existence, like sleeping, cooking,

bathing, studying and relaxing quietly after work. At an office or work place, specific activities are performed which, although they affect us directly, are conditioned by causes and effects that are far from our own personal concerns. This is different from a home. The treatment of the space within a house depends exclusively on the individual, and so requires a carefully thought-out plan that focuses on the distribution of the distinct rooms where various activities are performed, and the most efficient and proper connection between these rooms.

The first and proper estimate of the available space consists of creating a study of the surface area in two dimensions with a sketch or schematic diagram. This is only a simple drawing done in freehand with lines and arrows that indicate the passageways between the different spaces. It is nothing more than a simple, imperfect sketch of the true dimensions, but it is quite useful for starting to separate the most commonly used areas of the house from those that are more quiet and set apart. It is also used to decide where to locate the distinct zones of the house.

It is helpful to experiment with the various possibilities that the distribution of the rooms offer, and their relationship to and communication with the rest of the house until the most satisfactory solution is discovered that best suits the tastes and needs of the inhabitants.

Once the initial ideas are fixed, a more careful study should be undertaken of the home's organization, by creating a cross-section plan of the space with exactly proportioned dimensions for each room and their exact placement within the home. This plan or blueprint shall also establish the location of the doors or the dimensions of the hallways. This blueprint must be made to scale and traced on a paper to allow the different sizes of the rooms to be clearly seen.

Here, since there is no entrance hall, a room which, with the diminishing size of apartments has come to be considered unnecessary, the staircase has been used to screen the dining room from view upon entering to preserve a sense of privacy.

The living room, completely integrated into the kitchen / dining area, uses unique design elements such as the chimney and modern furniture that can be considered almost classic.

In this split-level, whose dining room, staircase and bedrooms we have already seen, the kitchen is also open to view, separated from the entrance by a panel rising only part of the way to the ceiling. It has a bar intended to serve as a daily eating area.

The next step is to make individual plans of each room in a larger scale, in order to be able to carefully determine the most appropriate distribution of the furniture and other furnishings for their proper use.

So that a plan can be representative of the available space and useful for the decorative tasks to be performed, the following items should be kept in mind and included in the plan:

• Supporting walls and non-supporting walls.

• Possible variations in floor levels.

• Electrical current and switches.

• Built-in cabinets and other fixed elements like chimneys, stairs or bathroom fixtures.

• The placement of the doors and windows and the direction in which they open.

• The location of the central heating and cooling system, if it exists.

As a final point, it is interesting to note that today a home can be acquired based solely on a plan, which is to say before it is even built.

A view of the staircase showing how the space under it has been used for a sideboard. This demonstrates how different styles can harmonize in one room, since this entire wall is modern while the opposite wall, shown in the photo above, contrasts with the use of an old mirror.

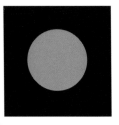

Mixed but not scrambled

A home is a group of rooms, each one of which is dedicated to a specific function. But in daily life there are domestic activities that are interrelated, and the distribution of the house reflects this reality. Consequently, homes are organized along the following lines: kitchen-dining rooms, dining room-living rooms, bedroom-bathrooms. The relationship between the kitchen and dining room in particular must never be forgotten when planning the design of a home. The food is prepared in the kitchen and served in the dining room.

The two rooms must be next to each other for quick and comfortable movement. It would awkward and tiresome to have to cross through a long hallway or through another room each time a dish is served or the table cleared. And this would not just be true for the family dinner. In a family of various members it would be aggravating when a fast breakfast is wanted before hustling off to work, or when the afternoon snack is prepared for the children. The era of servants, who were charged with preparing the meals and readying the tables is long past, and nowadays, with the wife frequently working as well as preparing the family meals, a lack of time begs the necessity for lessening the distance between the kitchen and the dining room. It is important, therefore, that there are modern and original solutions to the matter of proximity.

If the size of the kitchen is sufficient, a table and chairs may be installed there, creating a small dining area, to be used for breakfast, lunch and even quick dinners typical of working days. If the space doesn't allow for this option, there is always the possibility of using folding tables and chairs that can be stored away at the same time the kitchen is cleaned up after meals. It is important that means are taken to assure that the area is not an uncomfortable spot for eating, whether because the area

does not offer an attractive appearance or because it is surrounded by the normal disorder of kitchen work.

For studio apartments, where one room must suffice for the kitchen, dining room and at times even the bedroom, there is no other option but to install a low partition with a counter on top, the kitchen appliances unavoidably in view.

To escape the claustrophobic feeling that a limited space may provoke, to create zones or areas dedicated to the different domestic activities and to establish the sensation of a home, the kitchen area may be tiled with a distinct material. It will not compromise the sense of space. On the contrary, if will offer a nice decorative touch and will be a handsome addition.

When old warehouses or offices are rehabilitated for residential use there often times exist within the same large room specific zones for living room, dining room and kitchen. In these cases the tendency today is to leave the space open to keep it interesting. With more space, one can opt to separate the kitchen from the dining room with a low piece of furniture, or even, more simply, using different types of lighting. In any case, it is always preferable not to divide up the space. The sense of depth and width that these renovated buildings offer is always positive.

Finally, if in a living space both rooms are separated by a partition, it can be highly aesthetic to tear the partition down and substitute it with a wall of medium height, leaving a passageway open to one side. Another option would be to install some sliding doors that can be closed when desired.

The eclectic mixture of elements that characterizes this interior creates a rich visual feast.

Behind one of the sofas, a grand piano acts an elegant, aesthetic counterpoint.

Ethnic crafts and rich accent colours give this corner a distinctly exotic feeling.

A corridor lined with storage leads away to the garden.

Atmosphere

To achieve a good atmosphere in a room, or in the home, is the aim of all types of decoration and requires all the designer's knowledge. A different thing entirely are the various different atmospheres that make up a home, i.e. different areas which are necessary for different functions. There are three such areas in a conventional home: the bedroom and bathroom; the kitchen and storage space and the living areas, although there may be others such as work areas -offices - or rooms for social occasions, as part of a reception area. These areas should be isolated to as great an extent as possible and properly linked together.

Here we can find a clear connection between the idea of "atmosphere" and "atmospheres", because it is difficult to achieve a pleasant result when decorating an area which does not suit its purpose. This, which may appear obvious, is fundamental when considering a project for a new or refurbished dwelling. Interior design lends the final touch to an architectural structure, and a distribution of the interior space of the home; and a good end result - the atmosphere - is achieved via a suitable planning of the space. One of the most valid proverbs concerning decoration says that the essence of good interior design is the capacity to ask simple questions, and that good decoration is 98% common sense and 2% aesthetics.

The designer must familiarize himself with the requirements of the family and carry them over into his project before starting to focus on the decoration itself. An impractical space will never be successful, however well cared for it is.

When focusing on the decoration of each room, the idea of the focal point is all important. The main focal point is that which defines the function of a space: the seating arrangement in a living room, the table in a dining-room, etc. This main focal

point should be concentrated on, the rest of the room acting as a complement to it. In modern buildings, there are often spaces which need to fulfil a dual function, such as dining-living-rooms, or kitchen-dining rooms. The answer to this is a decoration which is dynamic enough to integrate the two spaces without creating a conflicting effect, a task which the interior designer constantly needs to face.

Together with the main focal point there are other, secondary ones which should be taken into account when planning the decoration of a room. The most common are:

• An empty space; a window or opening to the exterior, especially if it is a good light source or offers an attractive view.

• A hearth, which always attracts attention. The surrounding area is treated in accordance with the level of consistency or contrast we wish to create with the remaining space.

• A painting, collection of paintings, or a mirror. This is usually a focal point which combines perfectly with the main focal point; they may even become main points themselves, with the remaining decoration and furniture acting as complements. This can also occur with a "fine" piece of furniture, an artistic object of certain value. These features override the functionality of the room, which becomes a space for social interaction.

When planning a room, the greatest harmony possible should be sought between the main and secondary focal points. This is one of the key factors which explains the great progress interior design has made over recent decades: its flexibility, its capacity to produce dynamic effects, which can stem from a wide variety of uses. Furniture has barely changed over the past few centuries, even though current design is based on multi-functionality. There have been decisive changes, however, in the family itself,

Details in good taste, strategically positioned, are fundamental to finish off a decorative corner.

There are three different areas which make up this large living room, plus the bedroom. They are differentiated by the use of raised floor areas. This is a corner of the library which has been dealt with in this way to make it stand out.

This modern set of drawers has a balanced composition. The objects placed on top are two stone sculptures hose forms balance with the overall context to produce a harmonic whole.

in lifestyles and the in the size and structure of dwellings themselves. In this case, the decorator's or designer's knowledge needs to compensate for the characteristics of furniture whose basic forms need to be adapted to our present requirements, which demand greater dynamism. It is here we find the different solutions for ceilings, floors, perspective, light and color, patterns and textures.

Last, the conventional aim of the designer is harmony, although all decoration must be adapted to the character of the person living there to create a successful atmosphere.

Yet current interior design has overcome any apparent informality and even the capacity to surprise: the architect Sir John Soane defended random, unexpected forms of decoration: for example, leaving a large space via a small door in order to enter a cluttered space. It is not easy, but similar effects can be achieved by the interplay of light, moving from well-lit areas to other, shadowy areas, not forgetting the texture of the floor and the color of the walls. The key to attaining the "right" atmosphere is to know the requirements, to make rational use of the space, to have sufficient means and to take advice concerning the 2% aesthetics in the design process.

This is a fine example of how a loft is lived in. All the elements are susceptible to being changed around and the walls, here substituted by screens and curtains, can also be changed at will.

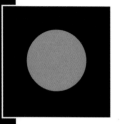

An exotic place

The world of decoration encompasses a wide range of possibilities and options, both in terms of style, color, type of atmosphere, distribution of elements, etc. It is infinite and capable of being adapted to any idea and satisfying the most extraordinary requirements. The exchange of contacts between peoples, a liberalization of tastes and the general modernization of society have instituted new fashions and other forms of decoration.

We have always been attracted by exotic items, but, such fascination has generally been associated with the decoration of somewhat eccentric and bohemian homes.

Normally, such aesthetic contributions have been limited to tiny complementary details, such as Persian rugs, Japanese futons or a few small African and Asian sculptures, whose beauty and convenience fit with any decorative style. The modernization of communication systems and the resulting cultural crossovers and, above all, the increase in tourism to distant places and contact between peoples of distinct mentalities has signified a new taste for things exotic and distant. The result of this is a decorative style in its own right. In effect, by decorating bedrooms, dining rooms or living rooms with exotic and enigmatic items has now become commonplace in the West.

In fact, nowadays, unlike many years back, it is no longer necessary to visit distant lands in order to buy these types of pieces and complements. There exists a multitude of stores where all manner of South American handicrafts, African cabinetwork and Eastern ornaments are sold.

Nonetheless, it is important to remember not to simply fill the house up with a collection of cliché souvenirs, but rather create an original and coherent atmosphere that is personal, looks comfortable and exotic.

This type of room must be simple in order to highlight the beauty of the colored and printed fabrics as well as the materials employed. Modern materials, such as plastic, methacrylate or treated metals should be avoided. It is preferable to make do with a few high-quality pieces that are original, rather than use imitations.

This type of decoration is perfectly apt for small spaces since we can do without certain pieces of classical furniture which tend to clutter the space.

Many rural handicraft objects, with their own particular fabrics and colors, and other genuine ethnic articles have a special charm. Handmade objects with simple forms and decorated with tiny motifs in their natural color lend a sensation of unique modern decoration to the home. There is a wide array of items to choose from: masks, African animal skins used as rugs or as upholstery for a sofa, hand-carved trunks used as lamp stands or auxiliary furniture, ornamental objects made of materials like ivory or native fabrics printed with lively colors and a stylish decoration that brings to mind adventure on the African continent. Finally, walls, whitewashed or painted with yellowish colors, warm greens or oranges, and wooden floors combine to create an atmosphere that must not be excessively over-adorned so as to preserve its primitive impact and visual force.

Colonial furniture, currently in vogue, is an elegant option. This style of furniture originated in India and South-East Asia. It is mainly manufactured from noble woods or wrought iron combined with natural fibers produced with artisan techniques.

Tables, chairs, rocking chairs, bottle racks, display cabinets or bedside tables, which are solid and resistent, are turned into extremely exquisite works of art brimming with exotic sensuality.

This general view shows how "anything goes" when the objects reflect the author´s personality. Exotic plants and flowers, books, diverse objects. This profusion of color, combined in harmony, fits perfectly with the warmth of the fabrics that cover the chairs. This type of decoration has impact, thanks to the light it doesn´t lose any of its attraction when, at night, it is illuminated by electric light .

Fabric of good quality, a display of exotic flowers and collected boxes combine to create a corner which is totally harmonic in color and materials

This almost chaotic living room is filled with life and personal memories. The objects, collected over a lifetime, speak for themselves. The atmosphere is completely informal, but within the apparent disorder lies a certain decorative balance and an underlying theme.

Another, versatile and imaginative economic solution is Rustic Mexican furniture. The pieces in this style are characterized by their lightness, but what they appear to lose in solidness they gain in the brightness and splendor. This type of decoration gives the room a warm, indigenous atmosphere that reminds us of sunsets and the colors of exotic birds and flowers.

These designer decorative elements are made out of wood, driftwood and plastic bottles. Together, these objects are harmonized by contrast.

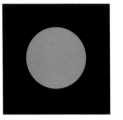

City eclectic

Today, as in the past, the conditions that life imposes affect to a large degree the decisions taken when building and decorating a home. In fact, high rental costs and mortgage rates for purchasing a house or apartment, along with the incurred maintenance costs of any home, take a large bite out of the family income. As a result, the range of possibilities for purchasing furniture and home furnishings is often quite limited. And so it is frequently necessary to improvise solutions that might seem a bit eclectic, taking advantage of sales and even at times secondhand items, to the detriment of beauty and stylistic unity. It is even common, given space restrictions, for many people to forego their aesthetic intentions, since it simply isn't possible to fit the desired furniture into the limited space available. Under these undoubtedly difficult conditions, the task of decorating a home is to strike the perfect balance between function and aesthetics, beauty and comfort.

We must forget the old stereotype that associates aesthetics with uselessness, function with the absence of comfort. Neither should one think that success in decorating is necessarily tied to a large economic outlay, or requires a professional decorator to guarantee the result. The success of an eclectic distribution of decorative elements in a space can be simply attained, capturing that subtle sensation one has when entering a modest home which, for all its simplicity, has been decorated with joy and imagination, showcasing a logical harmony that has been attained by a determined distribution of elements and a clear visual combination of objects, textures and colors that refer to different styles.

One good solution is to place a simple set of furniture in the home to center attention on the accessories or on paintings on the walls. The result can be an attractive union of old and new objects or of differing styles. The sense of unity is heightened if the tones of the entire living space are unified through, for example, the installation of the same type of flooring, the same background colors or similar lighting techniques.

All of this contributes in large degree to centralize the decorative leitmotif that governs the entire home. Along these lines, urban apartments and studios don't always have strong natural light, so it is helpful to paint the walls in soft, light tones. The use of low-standing furniture can produce a sensation of more light, as well as accentuating the breadth of the space.

Another option for urban spaces, which generally lack personality, is to infuse them with feeling and ambiance through the use of daring colors and unconventional textures, placing details that call attention to themselves and which break the monotony or 'gloom' of the environment. Habitually, these types of homes will have a functional set of drawers upon which a television is placed, a small, improvised coffee table, an old, inherited bed or an inexpensive sofa. Enlivening this monochromatic theme by painting these types of auxiliary pieces of furniture with bright colors like lime green or a strong red, or adding some lively and contrasting colored pillows to the sofa, will create not only an attractively modern setting, it will also significantly alter the atmosphere of the space and give the sensation that the area breathes.

All of this just noted is evidence that no great economic outlay is required. It is a matter rather of adding some details - they don't have to be many - so that the monotony and lack of personality that afflict so many of these types of apartments is broken. Urban apartments are constructed to maximize the limited space available. By using some imagination a truly pleasant and comfortable home can be created.

This other view of the bedroom shows even more disparate objects and furniture. Nonetheless, everything harmonizes and balance is achieved. The ceiling fan adds a touch of comfort and well-being.

Pastel tones such as the pink of one of the walls and the green of the other reflected in the mirror provide a good basis for enhancing any object. The dotted curtain adds a naive air. The white frame lends the mirror weight and consistency while the floor lamp provides an imaginative touch

The bordering stencils separating the two halves of the wall are easy to create and one of the best ways to provide a transition. The pinks and strawberry colors in the painting complete the colorful effect.

This personalized bedroom, filled with fantasy and imagination, looks like something out of a fairy tale.

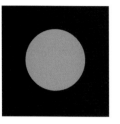

Sitting in elegance

The frenetic pace of modern life has transformed comfort from a basic human necessity into something subordinate to the intense rhythms of work and dependent on pressure and stress. As a result, anything that encourages relaxation and contributes to comfort and tranquility must be considered today as vitally important and desirable in any home. After a hard workday or returning from a trip far from home, you only want to disconnect and come home to a house that invites rest, relaxation and comfort in everything, down to the smallest details.

Aesthetic or decorative importance aside, no one can doubt the comfort of a cushion on a chair, sofa or love seat. The wide range of cushions and pillows available on the market attest to this, as much in design as in their size and form. But neither can it be doubted that a cushion also constitutes a highly decorative element that carries a great aesthetic effect.

There is nothing better than to be comfortably seated or sprawled among some good pillows and cushions that, at the same time, are original and bring a decorative harmony to a space with their textures, forms and colors.

Until just a few years ago, cushions were elements whose aesthetic qualities were considered of secondary or little importance. But the truth is that their possibilities for improving the decorative scheme of a room are endless, and virtually no one today dares to doubt that cushions and pillows can bring harmony, refreshing contrast and cheer to the decorative whole.

Cushions and pillows can be found in all models on the market. In fact entire stores are dedicated to selling them. Square and rectangular shapes are the most appropriate for living rooms, since they adapt themselves best to sofas and seats, while round pillows lend vitality and informality to bedrooms and guest rooms. Cylindrical forms are ideal as an informal detail in the baby's room, playrooms and recreation rooms.

The way in which cushions are placed in a room is also important, since a good part of their decorative function resides in their proper distribution.

Simply changing around their place, or substituting them for others can make one sofa seem like another. For example, to capture a formal and elegant effect, cushions can be placed on each side of a sofa in an ordered line. On the other hand, if they are placed on top of each other a more youthful and dynamic effect is achieved that is more informal and less calculated. The same holds true when placing pillows or cushions on a bed.

In general, pillows and cushions that are sold in stores are filled with polyester or down, but they can also be made at home. The advantage here is that the most appropriate fabrics, designs and colors can be selected and custom-made to fit into the decorative scheme of the house.

A smart combination of cushion textures can offer enormous decorative possibilities. A collection of cushions with solid colors on a sofa lend a classic and sober sensation, while cushions with a striped or checkered pattern will offer a more modern and, in a certain way, more informal appearance.

The most modern and practical way for closing a pillow is with a zipper, although they can also be closed with Velcro. In the latter case, keep in mind that if the pillows are overstuffed they might open up too easily.

In short, it is important to know of the infinite decorative possibilities that cushions possess. This includes the option of substituting them during the different seasons of year, to lend a room

In this environment, the color and touches of frivolity are the 100% responsible for the successful results achieved. It is indisputably a very feminine corner which has managed to strike the difficult balance of a decoration which verges on exaggeration.

Panther upholstery fits splendidly with 50's furniture. This armchair recovers all of its original splendor and charm when upholstered in this way. This type of upholstery, though, must naturally be used with measure as it is quite conspicuous.

A lack of color can be as stunning as a profusion of it. To achieve certain elegance, nothing can be more ideal than using only an interplay of black, grays and white.

an air of change or variation, so long as respect is maintained for the basic decorative tendencies of the environment as a whole and the piece of furniture where the pillows are placed.

There is no doubt that a cushion, being a simple, economic element that comes in multiple sizes, shapes and colors, can help us to change the aspect of a decorative scheme or even salvage the otherwise decorative limitations of a humble or outdated piece of furniture.

White and red are infallible, especially when the decorative elements are as austere and elegant as these. In fact, if we were to eliminate the red curtain, the space would lose all impact and personality.

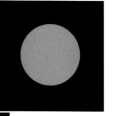

Color harmony and contrast

Everyone interested in decoration knows it is a subject that involves an interplay of a variety of elements, all of which are important. A perfectly decorated room is the result of a series of factors that when combined properly produce a perfect combination: the harmony of lines, proportions, the calculation of surfaces, colors, etc.

Even though this is one of the most subjective aspects of home decoration, color is by far the most important aspect since it transmits the sensation of place and lends unity and personality to the home. It is difficult to know why two people may have different feelings about the same tone of color, but one thing is certain: color is a decorative element that produces a physical and emotional reaction in the same way an individual perceives atmosphere. It is evident that the same decoration, with the same distribution of elements can change

When there is a potent predominant color like the red walls here, be they interior or exterior, the best solution is to paint the rest in a neutral color to compensate. The contrast can be highlighted with complements of a striking color.significantly by varying the colors.Before embarking on a decorative project, it is very useful to consider your own personal color and tonal tastes. Do you wish to create a simple atmosphere that produces a sensation of space or one replete with ornaments? Do you want a traditional or an informal design? Are you searching for tranquility or for an effect that will create impact. Each option requires the most suitable tonal ranges.

It is often the case that the persons themselves are not sure exactly what colors they like or what colors would be most appropriate for the type of atmosphere they wish to create. Doubtless, by examining some garments and other personal objects, they will discover some of their preferences and the

type of sensations they wish to create with the colors in question. It is truly surprising to discover how radically we can alter the appearance of a room or hide conspicuous defects by using the right colors. It all boils down to the fact that these colors have a close relationship with the balance of a room, a determining factor for carrying out the entire decoration process.

For instance, if your aim is to lend a new atmosphere to the living room, while at the same time retaining certain objects (a carpet, curtains, a sofa) of various colors, you only have to choose a color you find to be most pleasant and use it as your color base for decorating the whole. And if the immaculate white of the walls and the other elements appear to influence the atmosphere too much, just add a few notes of striking and lively colors, such as red and green, in order to avoid a monotonous and cold atmosphere.produce a great variety of emotions. The use of white to dark colors can produce tranquility and harmony, as they make a room appear smaller and lend it a sensation of seclusion. Nonetheless, such colors are never advisable for use in small rooms and those with little light. Very soft tones increase our visual sensation of space. Loud colors, such as yellow and scarlet, which, used their own, bathe a room with light and optimism.

A few discreet alterations in tone, in contrast, always produce an effective result: for instance, you want the predominant color of the room to be blue, it will not be necessary or even suitable to paint the walls and the ceiling in this color, as the result would be a room too dark. All that is required are a few "brushstrokes" (shelves, curtains, or a sofa) of the color in question in order to attain the desired effect.

As we have already mentioned, color can, by itself, It is important to remember that two or more colors, whether they are for

The color contrast between warm and cool tones, such as pistachio green and red, lends a sensation of breadth and brings out the architectural forms.

Seen from a different angle, we can appreciate how the white ceilings form a bond between the two colors of the two rooms, thus lending the whole coherence and common sense.

Here there is no problem of aesthetics when going from a room painted with striking green color scheme to one another painted with in a stunning tone of red; proof that by coordinating colors harmonically, it is possible to create daring contrasts.

contrast or harmony, can produce effects that are very dynamically different.

Thus, turquoise blue may appear excessive for objects or large surfaces, but, when combined in subtle details with white or green tones, its intensity is softened and once again becomes pleasant to look at. If you wish to lend vitality and cheerfulness to a rather cool-looking room, paint the walls with more intense colors like green or red. If you want to create a, tranquil and serene marine-like atmosphere, the softest tones of blue will have to harmonized with white, ochre or an umber color.

It is also important to bear in mind when you are deciding on the most suitable colors for the room you want to decorate, you should think about what it will be used for, as each tone influences our mood in a different way and, therefore, one color will more suitable in accordance with what the room is designated for. For example, a reading room will always require light tones like white, which induce peacefulness and concentration, while lively and striking colors in a child´s bedroom is fitting with the energy of its young occupant and will arouse his or her imagination.

In contrast with the red living room and applying the same color criterium, the bedroom has been painted an intense turquoise blue and, for motifs mentioned in the photograph on the following page, the ceilings have been left white

countryside, seaside, harmony and light

Atender a los esquemas compositivos capaces de conseguir
equilibrio en los volúmenes y ritmo en colores y tonalidades.
Dadas unas dimensiones y una estructura del espacio, y siempre teniendo
en cuenta la calidad de suelos y paredes, los volúmenes, los colores y la ilu-
minación son factores esenciales del equilibrio y de la armonía. De la adecua-
ción o no de estos factores dependerá la sensación que se perciba: comodidad, elegancia,
informalidad, saturación o incongruencia.

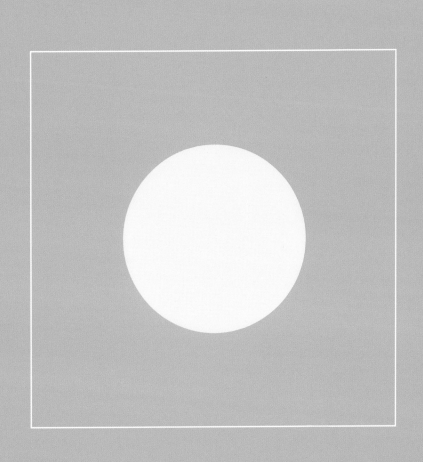

Spatial harmony

The size and shape of a room are often the primary factors in deciding where to place the most important pieces of furniture and accessories. Nevertheless, the relationship between the decorative elements as well as the space they take up can be equally important in the creation of a functional and esthetically pleasing arrangement.

The creation of a pleasant and practical environment requires the balancing of all of the elements used into a harmonious whole. A beautiful color scheme, for instance, can lose its charm if the dimensions of the room are not taken into account. Dark colors tend to make a room look smaller, and would therefore not be suitable for a room where space is a problem. In the same way, any piece of furniture can lose its beauty if it does not fit in stylistically with the rest of the furnishings or if it is badly lit.

In short, the following concepts can serve as a guide for finding a decorative arrangement that is not incompatible with practical or functional considerations.

Scale. The arrangement of a room will obviously have to take into account the size of the pieces that are going to be placed in it, but it should not be forgotten that many small details, such as decorative objects, can actually make a room look bigger.

A proper analysis of scale will not only take into account the physical size of the objects, since in decoration the visual effect is often more important than physical reality. A table will never give the same impression of bulk as a couch of similar size, since their scales are visually different. The best way to find the right combination is to experiment and trust your own impressions.

Balance. In order to produce a pleasant and balanced effect, size, color, lighting and function must all be taken into account when arranging elements in a room. The three most common kinds of balance are:

• Symmetrical. This implies choosing a central point of attention and positioning identical items symmetrically around it. This results in a focal point towards which people instinctively direct their eyes when they enter the room. This kind of arrangement brings peacefulness and stability to a space, but it is often difficult to achieve perfect symmetry in a room.

• Asymmetrical. In this type of arrangement, the objects that surround the center are similar but not identical. This can be achieved in two ways. Different objects with a similar visual impact can be placed at the same distance from the center. An example of this would be two similar, but not identical, night tables placed on either side of the bed. The other kind of asymmetry would to place two very different objects at different distances from the center.

• Radial. This kind of balance involves the circular repetition of objects around, towards or away from the center of attention. It is especially suitable for circular shapes, since its curved lines limit the available space in a square or rectangular room. Additionally, it is very useful for providing dynamic contrast, as in a wallpaper pattern, for example.

Rhythm. The proper placement of items is closely related to the concept of rhythm, which is based on a consistent pattern that can take on various forms:

1. Repetition: The most basic form of rhythm is based on the repetition of similar elements. It is pleasant and provides balance, but its overuse can be monotonous.

To create an atmosphere, a central decorative element should be chosen. This antique porcelain washbasin is the star of this corner. A useful marble shelf has been installed under the mirror on which to place accessories and complements such as small bouquets of flowers. The whitewashed walls and the wooden and wickerwork details lend a cottage air.

2. Variation: A pattern provided by alternating two or more elements in a sequence. This is more dynamic, but care must be taken to balance the style and size of the objects employed.

3. Progression: A gradual increase or decrease in colors or shapes. Tones, sizes, textures, materials, or lines can be progressively varied to produce this effect.

4. Contrast: The arrangement of two elements that differ in color, shape, or size so that the difference is obvious. Overuse of this technique can result in a loss of balance or harmony in the room.

A wardrobe has been placed in this corridor to break the linear monotony of this often unused space. The decoration consists of a basket of dried plants and a semi-circular wall lamp. The sienna color of the stucco and the Nordic blue create contrasting light effects.

A rectangular opening in the wall provides an interesting window, adding light and offering a display area for groupings of decorative objects. The result is one of balance and symmetry. The table, with Provençal touches and the teak chairs bring a note of color and informality.

It is shaded from the sun by foldable awning which creates a separate environment within the terrace area where cheerful deck chairs upholstered in maroon and decorative terra-cotta objects have been placed in a linear fashion to accentuate the wall. The earthen floor tiles and the ochre tones used create a certain rustic atmosphere.

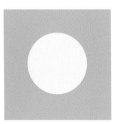

Sparkling light

Light is a fundamental element in the decoration of any house. In spite of this, it often fails to receive the attention it deserves. Effective illumination of a house involves regulating the degree of intensity within a wide range of possibilities.

Light can be softened or enhanced to create contrasts, which serve as a point of reference when arranging interiors. Adequate use of daylight has a great effect not only on the decor but also on our mood. The direction the windows are facing is the most important factor to determine how much daylight can be used without having to invest in expensive reforms. For this reason, it is essential to consider the number of windows and the direction they are facing before buying a new house or remodeling an old one. A house with plenty of daylight will change throughout the day, causing a variety of impressions and highlighting or hiding certain aspects of the decor.

Daylight has a profound impact on our visual perception of a space. It can therefore be a way to modify the appearance of a surface by using contrasts of shadow and light. A small room, for example, can be made to appear larger if we let light in through transparent curtains. If, on the other hand, we want to reduce the visual impact of a large room, this can be accomplished with heavy curtains and upholstered valances. The careful use of light can also hide uneven surfaces and make ceilings look longer or shorter.

Light and color.

No analysis of light would be complete without mentioning color, since two are inextricably united. Color cannot exist without light, and light can change the appearance of colors, making them more or less intense and bright. Because of this, light can create uniquely personal spaces with a variety of tones and colors. After all, a rainbow is just a breakdown of light, and the objects, furniture and finishes of a room only reveal their color when light reflects on them.

The colors of the spectrum take on different appearances depending on the intensity of the light that reflects on them. A Mediterranean house by the sea can almost appear to shine with its own light.

These houses are often decorated with bright colors such as yellow, blue, and especially white, which has the power to increase the luminosity of its surroundings. In northern countries, whites and pale colors absorb the weak light and multiply it, creating a discrete atmosphere.

We also perceive colors differently depending on the kind of light that reflects upon them. The same color can appear more luminous, pale, or intense depending on the type of daylight it receives. It would be no exaggeration to say the decoration itself is largely a question of playing this kind of shades and highlights off against one another.

If we take complete advantage of the available light, we can change the way the rooms of our house look. The use of white or pastel tones will make a room appear larger because of the way that these colors reflect light. A ceiling painted in light colors gives an impression of depth. If we want to make a room look smaller, browns and dark colors will do the trick, since they absorb light.

Windows.

Windows are the architectural component that allows daylight into a building. The way they are covered and decorated can alter the effect of the daylight.

A large bench decorated with blue molding is the centerpiece of this room, which features jute carpets and natural fiber chairs. The bright surroundings contrast with the dark wood of the end tables and accessories.

The ethereal curtain filters the light entering through this small window, lending the room a highly luminous effect.

The blue door and its frame stand out against the white-washed background, thanks to the light that comes in through the patio nearby. A spacious bench made of masonry acts as a decorative perch for colorful flowers, fruit baskets, and other decorative articles.

Translucent curtains provide a convenient way to soften light, although pleated paper can also be used for the same purpose. Wooden shutters have the additional advantage of being adjustable. This allows them to create a variety of effects by employing the contrasts between light and shadow.

Other ways to produce lighting effects include the use of transparent or opaque stained glass windows. Stencils can also be applied to glass windows to create attractive patterns of light. Skylights and other windows located high up on the walls are better left unobstructed to allow as much light as possible to enter. Other materials worth mentioning are opaque glass, pressed glass and pavés, which are all useful for softening and diffusing daylight.

This wall, whitewashed in the typical Mediterranean style, fills the room with light. The hyper-realistic painting in acid tones stands out against the white background, dominating the space. The radiant light fills the kitchen, highlighting the curtains covering the bottom of the sink.

A taste of the sea

Modern life is full of rushing, tension and stress. Especially in large cities, noise, the pressure of work and the countless problems of daily life and our dealings with people have created a constantly growing demand for rest and relaxation. This need for a place where we can lower our adrenaline and recharge ourselves for the next day has made home decoration increasingly important. By planning and arranging the decor to the smallest detail, we can ensure that our home is a relaxing haven, safe from the bustle of the outside world.

There are styles for every taste. Some prefer a modern, urban and eminently functional approach, while others prefer to create an atmosphere that recalls more idyllic environment, such as the country, the mountains, or the sea.

Most people would agree that the colors of the sea, the calm of a beach, or the activity of a harbor are surroundings that provide a feeling of peace which encourages rest and relaxation. It is not surprising, then, that many home-owners choose to decorate their houses with seaside motifs in an effort to forget the trials and tribulations of daily life. Although this option is perfectly reasonable, it is important to make sure that the house is suited to the style of decoration. Creating a seaside decor in a mountain house would seem shocking and illogical to most people. However, if the house is near the coast, or better still, has a view of the sea, this style can be most appropriate.

After a hectic day of work, or long day away from home dedicated to running errands of making social calls, the body and mind appreciate coming home to the comfortable and refreshing air of the sea.

Of course, creating such an atmosphere is not just a question of placing a few maritime objects around the room. However,

the task is not as difficult as some might think, as long as we take care to choose the correct materials for the furniture and choose bright colors that evoke the feeling of the sea. Finally, a few carefully selected objects, strategically placed, will add the finishing touches to the atmosphere.

In the living room-dining room, wicker is the most appropriate material for sofas and armchairs. Cushions in solid blue or white, or even blue and white stripes, can be placed on the chairs. Other elements that can add a seafaring flavor are natural wood window frames and doors, a raffia bench, or a round window opening onto the kitchen.

Decorative objects made of terra-cotta, or ceramics with pictures of fish, seashells, or starfish are also effective additions. Hobby enthusiasts can display their ship models to great effect, and pictures with maritime themes will be perfectly at home in this style of decor.

If the house has a balcony with views of the sea, it can be used for dining in the summer. A folding table made of wooden boards can give the impression of a seaside terrace. This can be combined with matching chairs with blue and white cushions.

In the bedroom, the wall can be painted indigo blue, ochre or yellow, or decorated with wallpaper with maritime motifs. These rooms are the perfect home for decorative objects such as seahorses, starfish or conch shells, which can be easily found on the beach.

A more daring approach is to pierce holes in the shells and string them into curtains, cushions, or even bedspreads. They can also be used as blinds or lampshades, especially for lamps with aquatic or maritime designs.

An old, whitewashed staircase decorated with antique tiles is the central element of this simply decorated space. Various seafaring accessories give the area its personality, such as a ship's lamp or the urn in the hollow space under the stairs. An antique wooden mirror and a jute rug add the finishing touches.

A traditional fireplace acts as the decorative center of this spacious living room. The various niches are used as shelves for displaying books and china. The masonry benches are covered with material that has an ethnic air, giving a touch of color to the sparse decor so characteristic of the maritime style.

Finally, the kitchen can easily be given a seafaring flavor by using wooden furniture painted in white or blue. Wicker fruit baskets can also be used to good effect, and the walls can be decorated with pictures of fish or other sea images. Brightly colored china or crockery can be left in full view to add a touch of color to the room. If the kitchen is big enough, a wooden table covered with an informal striped or checkered tablecloth will make it the perfect place to enjoy a relaxed meal of seafood.

Small decorative curtains are a good way to add a seafaring touch to a window.

This fireplace made of masonry gives us the opportunity to decorate the area with tools for tending the fire. The upper section of the fireplace has a niche which can be used as a practical bookshelf.

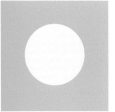

Attics with their own special charm

A house often has spaces that, because of their particular characteristics, offer a wide range of functional possibilities and decorative styles. One of these spaces which is often overlooked is the attic. Due to the lack of space which is increasingly common in today's world, this area, which can be found in both old and modern buildings, is often the only viable option when searching for additional living space.

The typical angled ceiling creates a natural play of lines and angles while a skylight adds a great deal of character. The unique charm of this type of structure lends itself to imaginative decoration, allowing for limitless contrasts and combinations. Perhaps the first image that comes to mind is the wooden construction. An attic, more than any other room in the house, is so versatile that it lends itself to rustic decor and classical or conventional arrangements which may evoke the past, creating an intimate or relaxed feeling, a bohemian or warm atmosphere. Moreover, since wood is often the original construction material, making the most of its qualities is the most aesthetically pleasing and economical way to bring personality or an original touch to an attic. An attic with bare wooden beams and wall panelling, with likewise wooden furniture and floors to match, is always comfortable and relaxing. It will also provide an atmosphere that is intimate and warm, two of the main characteristics of wood, and especially old wood, with its unique personality.

This is not the only possibility, however. The angles where the ceiling meets the walls can be highlighted with a stripe of paint in bright colors, which will stand out if the ceiling and walls are painted in the same color. If the beams are left unpainted, they can become another element of decoration by providing a repetition of color throughout the attic.

Another possibility would be to paint them so that they con-trast even more with the ceiling and add a note of elegance.

Here are some things the keep in mind when decorating an attic:

• Furniture should be kept to a minimum to preserve the impression of spaciousness while functional and practical solutions should be sought to the problem of storage.

• The floor of an attic may not be able to support much weight, so it might need reinforcement. In any case, the heavier pieces should be placed close to the walls whenever possible. Only relatively light pieces of furniture should be placed in the center of the room.

• Daylight is essential in avoiding a gloomy, claustrophobic atmosphere in this kind of room. Nevertheless, curtains or window shades can be useful for limiting the excess light which may enter the attic.

• Large lamps hanging from the ceiling are neither convenient nor decorative in this type of room. Strategically placed wall, floor or table lamps give much better results.

To sum up, a modern attic is no longer an oversized closet used for storing all kinds of knickknacks that will probably never be used again. Today it can be considered an extra room with just as many possibilities of use as any other, or even more. Here are some suggestions:

Study. This might be the most suitable use for this kind of room, since its isolation from the rest of the house allows the peace and quiet so essential for working or studying without interfering with the other residents. A spacious desk can be ideal for this, and the lower areas near the walls can be used for filing cabinets, drawers and shelves. If there is enough available

Attics often have stepped level floors. The floor should be covered in the same material to maintain unity. A warm wooden flooring or a soft rug can be of great utility. They are practical and can withstand weight like that of a chest, which can be used as decoration or storage space.

This bookcase was done by a sculptor and craftsman. It incorporates warmth and personality into its functional nature.

The only way to make an artistic area out of a bedroom cramped for space like this one is to use furniture cut to size, adding a sense of breadth through mirrors and light-colored walls.

space, a rug can visually mark off the part of the room designated for sitting and relaxing without having to resort to physical barriers that would destroy the feeling of open space.

Bedroom. Unless the attic is especially large, this calls for the use of few pieces of furniture, since the bed, placed near the wall, will normally take up most of the available space. The problem of lack of space can be alleviated by placing drawers under the bed, a chair for hanging clothes and a chest as a small wardrobe. If there is enough space for a regular chest of drawers, the drawer under the bed can be eliminated and a lower bed or even a mattress on the floor can be used instead, giving the room a more rustic or youthful look. In any case, the great advantage of using the attic as a bedroom is that it frees up a room in the rest of the house so that it can be dedicated to other uses.

Living room. While an attic is obviously not an appropriate place for a dining room, it can be a good place to relax and chat. In this case the room should have plenty of sunlight to cheer it up.

To make the most of the space available, the living room sofa here has been placed under a long window covered with bamboo blinds. The living room area is marked off by a brightly-colored hand woven carpet which separates it from the rest of the attic. Against the wall in a seemingly useless corner, a chest serves as a sidetable and display case for decorative objects.

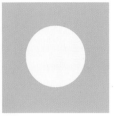

The simplicity of a cottage

The cottage style is a decorative form whose overall objective is to create an environment that exudes simplicity, relaxation and the tranquillity of life in the country. In contrast to the more strict rustic style, which bases its aesthetic value on the dominant elements of traditional rural homes (wooden beams on the ceiling, a chimney in the living room, and large wooden pieces of furniture,) the cottage style attempts to recreate in an urban setting the air of the countryside and the comfortable coziness possessed by these types of homes.

Regarding the division of space in the home, the principal idea necessary to keep the rural spirit alive is to assign only one function to each room. The living room must not be joined with the dining room, nor a studio with a bedroom or recreation room.

The objective is to decorate each room with furniture that will create a cozy feeling and the simple comfort of country environs, while taking a rest from the noise and frenetic rhythm of big cities. In the living room nothing should seem studied, and when the time comes to decorate it, keep in mind that the name living room implies its major function, which is to live there, to feel comfortable and relaxed. Wood clearly is the material that is most in harmony with nature and for this reason wooden furniture is always appropriate.

The bedroom must be austere, almost monastic in appearance. It is best to include only a bed with an attractive wooden or wrought-iron headboard and a small nightstand. An attractive touch would be to install wooden shutters.

For a kitchen in this style, it is appropriate to include traditional utensils which should be hung or placed in view, such as copper pans, antique pots, and all types of small containers. It might even be a nice decorative touch to leave the shelving open, so that the plates, glasses and even food containers are visible. On the other hand, all electric appliances should be hidden away as much as possible.

The most appropriate decorative style for the bathroom would be to refurbish some antique pieces, but if this is not possible, a four-legged bathtub may be installed, white wall tiles with a trim and rustic terra-cotta floor tiles.

To achieve decorative integrity in this style, the final touch is to place accessories and small details that refer to the countryside. Pottery, fresh and dried flowers, baskets made of natural straw or the like, iron doorknobs, a collection of porcelain, curtains and pillows with colors that evoke country living such as greens and blues, and checkered tablecloths will all contribute in an immeasurable way to produce the sense of well-being appropriate to life in the country.

One of the most difficult aspects is the lighting. It is clearly unthinkable to use only candles or oil lamps, but the electric lighting should be as concealed as possible. The illumination should in any event be soft and of low voltage. Some lamps made in a modern style, such as spotlights that focus up toward the ceiling are perfectly appropriate. On the other hand, patently false imitations of old lamps or candlesticks should be avoided at all cost.

If this type of decoration is desired, one must keep in mind several general observations which, if not followed, will bring the success of the decoration seriously into question:

This decoration demands treatment of the entire home. Do not consider merely decorating some rooms in this style and leaving other rooms in another style.

The combination of rustic style with Japanese elements lend this bedroom an air of personality and sophistication.

A staircase with a reflecting metallic handrail contrasts with the stone and wooden elements.

This futon is outfitted in colorful silk. A large tree trunk takes the place of a headboard, and the floor matts are marked off by long sticks of bamboo.

This type of decoration is difficult to successfully attain in a house with limited space.

If a cottage style is desired, keep in mind that it is expensive.

This type of decoration must exclude imitations. For the same reason, substitutes for authentic furniture, materials and ornamentation must be avoided. It is better to make do with fewer elements, but which are authentic.

The home must not be over-stuffed with things. Houses in the country are spacious and not filled with furniture. If this is to be recreated in an urban setting, which is always more limited in space, there is even more reason to be sparse with furniture and other decorative items.

A dark corner of the house has been converted into a useful dressing room equipped with wide wooden shelves. An ideal solution for eliminating bulky armoirs and heavy chests of drawers.

*In this corner, a small stainless steel washbasin,
with a unique and practical towel rack in the form
of a metal bar, has been placed next to an unvarnished
wooden wall. An opening window and a mirror complete
the decoration. Functional spotlights have been placed
on the beams for lighting.*

*A practical tubular toilet in stainless steel has been pla-
ced in a corner of the bedroom. The wall is hand-painted
with dramatic color contrasts. A bull's-eye above the toilet
provides natural light for the shower.*

*A wood panel floor and a ceiling with old beams can provide an informal atmosphere
similar to that of pub. The bare stone walls accentuate this effect even more. A table
for six with a wooden top, metallic chairs and movable spotlights on railings lend a
certain rural flavor to the whole.*

Taste, bathrooms and accesories

The rustic kitchen is based on several inevitable elements and materials: wood, china, glistening copper pots, terrazzo floors and solid, sturdy furniture. Although this style of decor gives the impression that it is made to last several generations, it has managed to adapt itself so that it still fits in nicely with the latest appliances that are part of the practical, modern kitchen.

The flavor of old recipes

Kitchen work often requires dedication and a certain disposition. Nonetheless, an adequately sized, beautifully decorated kitchen is always an invitation to start cooking. It is difficult to resist the temptation of preparing some delicious meals when the kitchen is large and cozy, and its appearance evokes the charm of a traditional rural home, where food preparation wasn't just a pleasure but an art. In fact, the rustic style goes wonderfully in kitchens, but sufficient space is essential. To attempt to adapt a rustic decorative style to a small modern kitchen will result in an unaesthetic and cluttered environment with an effect that is contrary to that intended. The dominant focus of the rustic atmosphere should be a large, central table that can be used interchangeably as a family breakfast site, a relaxed area for serving dinner far from the noise of city life, and as a supplementary counter when preparing meals. The rest of the furniture, preferably made of wood but which can also be made of Formica, laminates or glass, should consist of cupboards, shelving, closets and perhaps some traditional small wall units for storing cookies and other sweets.

Aesthetically speaking, even though it will mean more frequent cleaning, it is advisable that certain items such as porcelain plates, terra-cotta earthenware or old jars should be visibly displayed. The agreeable sensation of an overflowing bowl of fresh fruit, an artisan's basket full of bread, or the interplay of spice bottles all in a wonderful and studied disorder should not be ignored.

An attractive warmth is also added to the kitchen if saucepans, whisks, wooden bowls, frying pans, copper pots and other utensils are hung from a wooden bar and not stored away. However, the comfort of an environment that captures the bucolic and pleasant rural lifestyles of past eras should not be equated with a lack of modern technology. One original solution is to camouflage kitchen appliances such as the cooking range, the refrigerator, the dishwasher and microwave with panelling or surfaces that mimic the cupboards. There are appliances on the market that incorporate these very surfaces with the specific intent of heightening the rustic look.

The sense of nature and country living can be additionally established by painting the walls with warm, natural colors like beige, pale yellow, ochre or sandy brown. The general sensation of a natural setting can be completed with a tablecloth of thick linen in checkered patterns of white red, blue, green, yellow or brown, and various flower arrangements or potted plants.

Tiling in place of painted walls is a common form of decoration in the rustic style. Tiles are long-lasting and offer a wide range of decorative possibilities, as they can come with pretty trim or even be authentic, hand-painted artisan works.

Purists who desire their kitchens to exude the authentic atmosphere evoked by country homes, where almost everything derives from an active and artisan-like domesticity, often include original and attractive options which can, unfortunately, be expensive. Installing wooden beams on the ceiling, a typically traditional bread oven, or an open fireplace for cooking with wood are some frequent additions. A wooden framed opening can also be made in a partition between the kitchen and dining area, creating a practical counter for passing plates and transferring food from one room to another.

A set of wooden shelves can be an economic and striking solution to the problem of food storage in the kitchen. The food should be placed in a decorative fashion.

The work area in this rustic kitchen has been divided into three zones: a conventional stove cooking area, the washing area consisting of a stainless steel double basin sink, and a counter space for working. The modern functional cabinets and stainless steel counter contrast with the Catalan arched ceiling and the terra-cotta tiled floor.

A small rustic cabinet for storing spices and a decorative corbel are the key elements in this corner of the modern kitchen shown. A long curtain partitions off the kitchen and provides a relaxed country air.

If the walls are made of brick, these can be left in view to provide a rural atmosphere. If in addition, wooden floorboards are installed, shelves are hung and a wooden table is decorated with rustic complements and a warm lighting, the effect will be a pleasant and inviting space.

The heart of the home

If we want our living space to be transformed into a home, that is to say, a warm and cozy place to live in the most relaxed and comfortable manner possible, then as much importance lies in how we impose our own personality and lifestyle on the space as in the layout of the space itself.

To attain the former, it is essential that each room, each element, each detail is studied and considered carefully and lovingly. Just as we must dedicate ourselves thoughtfully to the decoration of the bedroom, the dining room and the living room to assure that they are designed according to our personal tastes and needs, so we must take the time necessary to properly decorate the kitchen.

Our personal stamp must be placed on everything to assure that the result will be a comfortable and enjoyable space to carry out the specific tasks pertaining to food preparation, no matter how small the kitchen may be.

Because of the various activities carried out in the kitchen, the quantity of items found there, and the tendency for the place to be in a state of disorder at various times during the day, the kitchen is one of the most complex areas in the house. As a result, it is also one of the most difficult to decorate successfully.

Modern ideas of interior design, adapting themselves to constantly changing culinary habits, the continual arrival of new electric appliances, and the incorporation of women into the modern-day work force has forever left behind the absurd and outdated notion which associates a kitchen with a small, dark and uncomfortable place, albeit, paradoxically, that it is one of the most utilized spaces in the house.

Naturally enough, there are individuals who consider slaving away in a kitchen to be of secondary importance, just as there are others who enjoy preparing food quietly and carefully according to preferred recipes in an atmosphere that evokes a natural, country setting, and still others who prefer a small and functional kitchen for the few moments they spend in the house or whenever they decide to eat there. Depending on space limitations and personal considerations, kitchens are normally intended to serve three distinct functions:

• A place for solitary chefs who prefer to pursue their art in peace and intimacy.

• A place to eat breakfast and maybe a quick meal or snack.

• A veritable family reunion site, where everyone eats, works and enjoys family conversations together.

In each case, even if mere functionality is desired, it is important to create an environment with a distinctive style that responds to the culinary needs of the users. Here are some options:

Country style. By using furniture, naturally colored wood, some rustic tiling and traditional utensils, the intent is to evoke the lighting and tranquillity of a country-style kitchen.

Mediterranean style. This style emphasizes the importance and beauty of simple traditional objects and frequently-used utensils over modern electrical appliances. All that is necessary for cooking is the ingredients, some good, sharp knives and functional pots, frying pans and bowls. The warm quality offered by a good wicker breadbasket or some antique wooden shutters on the windows is often surprising.

Urban style. This is a functional kitchen that takes the ultimate advantage of modern appliances and where everything is perfectly organized to facilitate meal preparation for those indivi-

Wood, metal and glass: three highly modern materials used to decorate an old warehouse

A large room has been turned into a functional kitchen situated in the center of a large work and cooking area over which a decorative hood has been placed. The beams are used as supports for hanging a variety of objects, such as pots and pans.

If space allows, an island can be placed in the kitchen as a work zone and bar area for informal eating. The winding wooden counter was carved by a craftsman. This and the ventilator hood in broken tile in the Catalan Art Nouveau style give the kitchen a unique look.

duals who are rarely at home or who are little disposed to spend time in the kitchen.

Industrial style. This style is a mixture of high-tech with an aesthetic quality appropriate to industrial locales; metal furniture, steel sinks and cabinets, synthetic flooring, etc.

Medieval style. This style is dominated by a few pieces of antique furniture and an appearance that offers a sensation of vitality and color. Fabrics that evoke past epochs, clay pottery and decorative flowers are essential for the quality appropriate to this environment.

Informal style. This style offers a youthful and jubilant appearance, happy, free and colorful. The cupboard doors and shelving, and even the appliances, are covered in bright colors, with forms that are unusual, original and amusing.

The sideboard and table have also been specially designed for this kitchen to give it a very personal and warm feeling. These are original hand-made pieces.

Kitchens with charm, flavor and color

A kitchen that is attractive, practical and well-organized is what makes cooking a pleasure rather than a drudge. So it is important to think carefully about the best way of distributing the space, especially if the kitchen is of a rustic nature, a type whose design is antiquated and which requires modernizing.

The most important aspects to aim for in a rustic decoration are coziness and quality. The main idea is to remember that the kitchen was once the dwelling´s central room. In order to achieve this, manufacturers now produce rustic kitchen furniture with natural-looking noble wood finishes with glass doors, through which the shelves can be seen. Nowadays, aesthetically simple lines are favored, without intricate ornamentation or moldings, combining synthetic finishes of bright cheerful colors with natural woods. In terms of wood, the most popular colors at present are natural, stripped and dyed, in oak, cherrywood, beech, etc. All woods used in the manufacture of kitchens must be treated with special varnishes that prevent dampness from setting in and preserve the heat.

One of the most important parts of any kitchen are the work surfaces. They must be resistent so they can withstand the work to be carried out on them.

The worktops must be able to withstand cuts, heat, dampness, grease and corrosive products. In other words, the surface must be highly resistant. In this case, wood also provides the best quality and the most pleasant choice. The problem with wood is that it is a delicate material, although this can be solved by creating little areas of steel, marble or a reinforced type of wood for the areas that are used most, thus protecting the worktop. Granite is another option. This is very appropriate due to its resistance to all manner of harsh bangs and abrasive products. Marble is also resistent to wear. The most commonly-used mar-

ble in rustic kitchens is white country marble. A current trend is to use steel worktops which produce a contrast with the rest of the rustic decoration.

With these examples we have tried to show all the possibilities that a rustic style decoration can provide. A kitchen, for instance, can combine wood in its natural tone with watery-green-colored tiles, stainless steel and polyester-lacquered finishes in white, as long as you know how to integrate these materials with taste.

Many ideas can seem very peculiar on paper, but when put into practice, surprise us for their outstanding decorative result. Another example is a design kitchen whose furniture is made of stripped and dyed solid wood, with a waterproof finish.

An elegant appearance can be achieved by playing with the extractor hood, which could be made of anything from steel and copper, to brick, to one painted with washable decorative paints, etc. For this reason it is essential to learn how to combine this with the furniture.

We have also reproduced different floors, since nowadays there are treatments so perfected that even parquet can be laid in cooking and work areas.

Likewise, furniture made of noble wood such as solid oak can be installed, so long as it has been treated beforehand.

Doorknobs also play an important role. Sometimes all that is needed is to change them for another type made of porcelain or wood and another material that combines with the worktop in order to increase the aesthetics of the kitchen. The decoration is often sustained by tiny details that can be considered the salt and pepper of a room.

Modern rustic design is currently in vogue. A large work bench made of Nordic wood makes for an excellent decorative element. The wall painted in a warm tone highlights the wood and gives the room a touch of elegance.

Taste, bathrooms, accesories

A small traditional kitchen with an old built-in ventilator hood with a wooden edge. It has plenty of room for working and hanging pots and utensils. Light enters through a frosted glass window.

Craft tiles are back in fashion and lend large country kitchens character and color. This room has been divided into two perfectly differentiated zones thanks to part of a former wall that juts out slightly, separating the zone containing the kitchen sink from the rest of the kitchen. Maximum advantage is taken of the space between the beams to hang pots and pans. This highly decorative style is common in rural homes.

An annex to the kitchen has been transformed into a practical pantry with metallic shelving. The large wooden closet lends the area a touch of mystery.

128

This closet with transparent doors has many shelves on which to place dishes and glasses. It has been placed in a corner behind a door to make the most of available space.

The washing area consists of a large marble sink and a cross-shaped faucet which provide an antique air. Small shelves are a good idea for leaving crockery and complements in sight.

This kitchen has been covered in Arabic-style tiles which contrast with the classical counter made of Italian marble with a scored edge. The collection of bottles and other objects in the corner adds a touch of color.

Alluring nooks and crannies

Storage and beauty don't often go together, especially in modern apartments where the lack of storage space makes it necessary to leave aesthetic considerations aside in favor of practicality.

However, every house has small, hard-to-decorate places that can be put to good use with a little imagination. Have you ever stopped to think that you could make an attractive and practical space out of an empty corner in the living room, a long-forgotten space under the staircase, a narrow hallway, or an inconvenient window that seems to be wasting precious space in a corner?

These places are often underestimated because they seem unsightly at first glance, and because the decorating process is generally concerned with the larger, global look of the house. When arranging the furniture in a living room or bedroom, for instance, we seldom stop to think about the small nooks and crannies that are left over.

These areas are usually accepted with resignation and left out of the decorating scheme. Ironically, the end result of this is that the rooms are overcrowded because of the wasted space. This necessary space can be found by taking a careful look at the house and using your imagination. Not all houses are the same, of course, but at least some of the following ideas should be of help in finding these spaces and putting them to good use.

Windows. These are very useful if they have a sill, which can be used for decorative items, such as plants or flowers, or as a practical shelf for books or other objects. If a window is located in a corner, it can make an ideal spot for a small work table with plenty of sunlight. If the corner is too small for a table, a decorative plant can take advantage of the light and add a cheerful touch to the room.

Two-in-one. There are many imaginative two-in-one furnishings on the market that fulfill both decorative and practical needs. Some examples are hollow lift-top benches or old trunks, as well as beds or wardrobes that have extra storage space on top or underneath.

Front hall. This part of the house already has multiple uses, such as entering and leaving the house and providing access to different areas. However, in addition to its importance in giving a good first impression of the house, it is also an ideal location for a tall, narrow closet or a small cabinet for storage.

Hidden corners. There is always wasted space in house that can be put to good decorative or practical use. Some examples are the space under a staircase, the back of a sofa or armchair that can't go flush against the wall or window, or the empty corner between two sofas. Floor lamps, plants or small tables and cabinets are especially suited to these locations. For example, practical shelves made of brick or wood can be built in the spaces at either side of the fireplace. A mini-bar is a possible alternative if there is a lack of space.

Just as the distribution of the house is based on size, proportions and individual needs, there should also be small, surprising areas that show off the versatility of the rooms while at same time performing a practical function. The ideas given here might seem superfluous, but they undoubtedly bring personality and originality to household decoration.

A landing can be the ideal place for a colorful flower arrangement, transforming the area into a focus of attention. The Nordic-style wood panelled wall is decorated with a straw hat.

A small stone washbasin adds personality to this corridor. The flowers function as a dynamic element within the sober decoration.

A small alcove between a closet and a wall has been transformed into a useful washbasin area. Tiling has been added to the walls to protect them from moisture.

In one corner of the attic, a custom-made chimney has been built and hand painted. It functions as both a decorative element and a source of heat.

Imaginative solutions in small bathrooms

An old house, a young couple looking for their first apartment, too many family members for too few square feet of living space, a small studio for a single person who has just moved away from home - most of us have been through experiences like this or know someone who has. Space limitations are part of modern life, and are often most apparent in the bathroom, which is usually assigned the leftover space after the other rooms have been laid out.

When faced with small bathroom (or kitchen), an imaginative arrangement of the essential elements can result in a small but cozy and functional room that satisfies the main household needs. The solution is not always easy, but can usually be found through two main methods: structural remodeling or redecoration. The former involves changing the actual structure of the room and its furnishings, which can often be expensive and difficult to perform without completely destroying the current structure and furnishings. If this is the case, the only alternative is to rearrange the space as efficiently as possible.

Obviously three basic elements: the toilet, washbasin and bathtub or shower will need to be accommodated, but the placement of the other furnishings should be carefully considered to take advantage of unused spaces. Some can even be eliminated if they are not strictly necessary: the bidet, for example, can be easily substituted by the bathtub or shower.

Storage space will inevitably be a problem. This can be alleviated by storing some items, such as medicine, extra towels, some cosmetics and the scale, for example, outside the bathroom. Disorganization, which is always bad, becomes even worse in these circumstances, since it wastes space and makes the

room look even smaller. Here are a few tips that can help solve this problem:

• There are invariably 'dead spaces' which can be put to good use in a small bathroom: the back of the door (for a towel or clothes hanger); the window sill (for decorations, a soap dish, a sponge, shampoo, or bath salts); the edge of the bathtub (for a metal rack holding the bath necessities) or under the washbasin (for extra towels, soap, toilet paper, scale or slippers). Shelves can also help to gain valuable space and can be covered with doors, like a cabinet, or more economically, with curtains matching the decor of the room.

The mirror can be the door of the medicine chest over the washbasin, rather than a separate element. This in turn can be used to store cosmetics, combs, brushes and shaving items. Free space can also be found under or on top of any fixed piece of furniture, such as cabinets or even the toilet.

• Mirrors on blind walls can increase the feeling of space. Limiting the number of colors to two for the furnishings produces a similar effect, as does using matching colors for walls and the towels.

• The shower basin can be covered with a false floor which can be raised or lowered to create more space. This can compensate for a lack of space in front of the washbasin.

• In a small bathroom, the whole floor should have more than one use: as an access to different areas, as a corridor, and as standing or sitting space (in front of the washbasin or around the toilet, for example).

A soap dish, towel rack and toilet paper dispenser have also been installed. The upper wall has been decorated with a mirror, antique wall lamps and some paintings to match.

A decorative mosaic
has been placed on
the shower floor.

*A gilt-frame mirror which was an old family heirloom
brings a classic touch to this avant-garde bathroom with
its ceramic washbasin, black marble countertop and convenient stainless steel towel rack. The atmosphere is softened by a discrete note of blue.*

*Very small ceramic tiles can dress up any bathroom corner.
They are practical, durable and stand out against the white
marble counter of smooth lines. The mixer tap adds a touch of
avant-garde to the atmosphere. An intelligent solution: separating the shower area with a clear glass partition.*

- In an old house it might be a good idea to install a new washbasin, toilet and bathtub or shower. The modern models are usually smaller as well as more comfortable. In any case, they will work better and brighten up the room.

- If the room is long and narrow, mirrors on the side walls will make it look wider. A cheaper alternative would be to cover the walls with tile.

- If the furnishings are the same color as the walls, they will look smaller.

- A checkerboard pattern in black and white will also make the room look larger. This can be done with the tile on the floor, for example.

*Clusters of perfumes and oils have been placed in studied disorder to decorate the
area. A painting with a wooden carved frame hung over the stuccoed, moisture-resis-
tant wall brings a note of color and light*

An antique framed mirror contrasts with the modern tile and built-in washbasin. Another classic touch is provided by the dual-handled faucet with old-fashioned, cross-shaped knobs.

The classic mosaic style is used to great effect in this colorful washbasin, which features a practical lower cubbyhole for storing towels. The multi-colored tiles and hand-painted mirror frame add the finishing touches to this bright and informal corner.

This bathroom features a cutting-edge design which integrates traditional and modern styles. Some of the outstanding aspects of this design are the multicolored tiles combined with mosaic, as well as the toilet which hangs suspended in mid-air and the colorful shower curtain.

Light and warmth in the bathroom

When organizing a living space, the first thought is to consider those rooms that will occupy the prominent positions in the house, such as the living and dining rooms, the master bedroom, etc. Other rooms are invariably left for later.

It is normal custom to assign the location of the bathroom at the very end, after having previously determined the various functions of the rest of the space. As a result, the bathroom is usually an interior room with hardly any available natural light. If it does have a window, it is often small, and little or no natural light enters. The window often opens onto nothing more than a ventilator shaft.

Depending on their dimensions, windows can be invested with various decorative treatments by using curtains, distinctive types of blinds (rolled fabric of various colors, wooden latticework, or small plastic, metal or bamboo blinds) or translucent shades.

Another option is to do without these window coverings, opting instead for the installation of frosted glass or wooden shutters appropriate to the rustic decorative style.

Windows can also provide some storage space. Small shelves, perhaps of glass, can be hung from their frames or the sills themselves can be used.

Artificial light is a basic theme for the agreeable utilization of a bathroom. The combination of direct points of focused light with general, indirect lighting is suitable to create a serene and cheerful atmosphere.

Spotlights embedded into the ceiling emit a whiter light than hanging lights. Their disadvantage is that the light they emit tends to too harsh.

Mirrors are also recommended since they increase the brightness in the bathroom by reflecting light, and also because they make the space appear larger. It is essential to hang at least one mirror over the bathroom sink, an area that must be well-lit. This is often performed with a pair of lamps to either side of the mirror or with some decorative light bulbs around the perimeter of the mirror, much like the style of a theater dressing-room. These lights should always be white, since colored lights, even if softly tinted and perhaps decorative in some cases, will compromise the mirror's primary function.

An important question relating to electric light is safety, since the combination of water and electricity is always dangerous. To avoid problems or accidents, we note here some pieces of advice that we consider useful and which will encourage taking proper safety precautions.

• It is advisable that light switches, at least those for general lighting, are installed outside the bathroom next to the bathroom door, since this will make it more difficult to touch them with wet hands.

• The wall sockets installed in the bathroom should never be near faucets or running water.

• Electric heaters, at times vitally important during the winter months or cold weather, should be activated by a cord so that it is not necessary to touch the appliance itself.

One area of this bathroom has been equipped with an ergonomic porcelain washbasin and four symmetrical mirrors lit by tulip-shaped lamps. The wooden bench provides a convenient place to store accessories and complements. An armchair upholstered in terry cloth and some floral arrangements add the finishing touches to the scene, which is illuminated by the reflections from the lemon-yellow tinted walls.

This restored antique iron bathtub and faucet with porcelain handles bring back reminescences of the renowned turn-of-the-century spa resorts.

When the case is a small guest bathroom, there are many ways to obtain a practical and aesthetic result within a very confined space. Light elements can live alongside one of a colorist and minimalist nature. A stainless steel basin fitted into a red synthetic surface and a touch of detail in the form of a white flower produce a Japanese atmosphere.

• It is important that entering a bathroom during cold weather isn't torture. Undoubtedly the most practical solution is to install a central heating system, but if this is not possible, an infrared heater can be installed above the door or mirror.

• An original appliance that could be quite useful is a heater-towel rack, which is an electric radiator that is also used as a place to hang towels. Warm towels can be a welcome relief in the winter months.

The recycled washbasin is made of pink marble and is attached to the wall with wrought iron supports. The marble surface has been adapted in order to hold this very modern washbasin. The wall is painted pale pink to match the marble. The floor is tiled with geometric bath tiles. The background wall has been covered with strips of pinewood painted neutral white.

Doubles spaces, vestibules and organization

Lofts currently very fashionable. The trend of turning them into dwellings allows us to take maximum advantage of the square meters available by creating mezzanines and split-level residences, in which some of the rooms have views to others. Furthermore, the need to take advantage of the space has compelled interior decorators and architects to find a way to get the most out of what was previously considered as transit zones, such as entrance halls and vestibules.

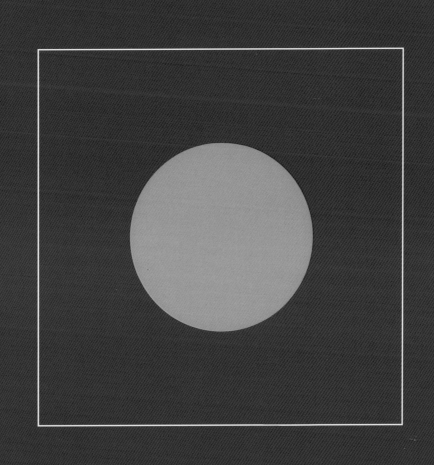

Not so long ago it was customary to reserve a room exclusively in the house for a library. The walls of the room chosen for this purpose were furnished with shelves and bookcases up to the ceiling. Also included were a desk and other complements so that the room could be used as a study or reference library. Nowadays, this practice is less common, especially due to the lack of space of current-day dwellings. The library has become something exclusive to literature readers or to certain professionals: teachers, journalists, writers, etc., who choose a room for working in or for pursuing their favorite pastime.

Nonetheless, nowadays most people continue to regard books as very attractive and decorative items in themselves, as well as the pleasure produced by a large variety of colors, sizes and textures, to such an extent that a room without books is considered highly unusual and can give the appearance of a barren space. Why is this, when one can purchase decorations that imitate the spines of books? And why are famous people always photographed in front of their bookcases?

If your house does not have a room for a library, the next best thing is to install it in a study, if you have one, or in the living room.If you are not an avid reader, you can place your books on a shelf or a piece of furniture in the living room, thus combining them with other decorative elements. However, if you do want to put up a small bookcase, any wall that is free will do.

Clearly, the bookcase is a piece of furniture that, due to its volume, can cause problems of space in a small dwelling, but that does not imply that it should be automatically excluded, since there are many ways of getting round this problem.

Before installing a bookcase, you should locate all the "dead spaces" in your home, such as a section of wall between two

windows, a free space on either side of a door or even the part that is available above it. In addition, the sides of a chimney may be interesting for placing shelves for use as a bookcase. It is worthwhile mentioning that there is a variety of systems comprising shelves or modules that can be fitted together, which allow a bookcase to be constructed according to the space available.

Don´t be frightened of filling a wall with books since, apart from any cultural consideration, they are very aesthetic and help to create a pleasant and cozy atmosphere. It is possible that long rows of books may produce a feeling of claustrophobia or oppression, but this sensation can checked by placing various decorative objects between books such as flowers, photographs, ceramics, a sculpture, a musical instrument, an antique of some kind, etc.

A television or a music system are ideal elements to place on a bookcase and thus prevent an overwhelming atmosphere. If there is enough space, the bookcase can also be used to separate two rooms, for instance, the living room and the dining room; or in a small apartment containing only one room, for separating the sleeping area from the rest of the space.

The material most widely-used is rustic, painted or lacquered wood that can be adapted to all manner of decorative styles, but you can also choose metal or methacrylate, for instance, provided it fits in with the general aesthetics of the room.

The most recommendable way to illuminate a bookcase is to use small separated and half-hidden spotlights placed between the books and objects. The idea of concentrating all the books in one area or in one bookcase can be reassessed, especially if you don´t have many books, or, even if you do have many, the space in your dwelling is limited and you cannot afford to use an

A light-filled room, designed in a highly functional way. There are virtually no accessory elements or ornaments. So, for instance, there are no curtains, something unusual. The entire decoration is based on lines, the upholstery of the furniture and the smooth color of the walls, interrupted only by the presiding painting. The books, stored on a sober and light bookcase, comprise a first rate decorative element.

Books are great allies in decoration. There is never a hostile atmosphere where they abound. This also applies to small apartments, although it is difficult to keep the shelves tidy in such a small place, since they are generally used to store other items, too.

A bookcase of a modern design often provides a practical and highly aesthetic piece of furniture, as the design aims at obtaining maximum capacity within a minimum space, in addition to the emphasis placed on materials and finishes.

entire room for them. Small groups of books, classified and selected carefully, distributed in various places around the house, as well as being attractive and decorative, prevent any oppressive sensation that can happen when a large quantity of books, are stacked in a single space. As was mentioned earlier on in this section, the books should be distributed in a logical manner in the dwelling´s different shelf space. For instance, art books and illustrated books, can be kept in the living-dining room; children´s books on a attractive and lively shelf in the children´s bedroom; adult books or those dealing with more reserved delicate subjects, in a small piece of furniture in the master bedroom; cook books should go on a shelf in the kitchen; novels and non-fiction books should either be placed in the entrance hall or in the passageway, on a low shelf on which other decorative items can be kept as well.

Although this clearly depends on the space available, there are always many solutions to get round this obstacle.

This is an austere bookcase. It is an ideal place for books to stand side by side with travel souvenirs, ethnic sculptures or any type of exotic collection.

Space to move

Hallways are usually the last part of the house to be considered when decorating. Although all of us pass through them countless times every day, we seldom stop to think about the many possibilities they offer. More often than not, they are left barren to serve their main purpose: to connect different parts of the house.

For economic reasons, or because of the difficulties in finding a pleasant way of decorating its long, narrow shape, this part of the house is often entirely forgotten when decorating the house. This mistake can deprive the house of an additional attraction which, considering how often it is used, could make a significant difference.

Since there is often a shortage of space in modern homes, it can be useful to consider the practical uses that a hallway can be put to. Some experts in decoration even think that keeping clothes in the bedroom is old-fashioned and detrimental to rest, and therefore recommend using the hallway as a dressing room.

Although this may seem extreme, an alternative could be to build a storage space from the top of the hallway to the ceiling which could be used to store clothes for another season. Shelves with items such as bottles, decorative figurines or plants can also save space while at the same time adding a personal touch to the house.

A small piece of furniture or even a shallow bookcase can be placed in the corridor, as long as they don't block the way or make it look crowded.

Of course, hallways are often too narrow for any of these uses. In this case, practical considerations must be left aside in favor of an effort to bring personality and beauty to this often neglected part of the house. Here are some suggestions:

• A carefully planned lighting arrangement can produce surprising and imaginative effects.

• Strategically placed mirrors can increase the feeling of space.

• An interesting idea for art lovers could be to use the corridor to house their art collection. Small spotlights directed at the paintings will produce the effect of a miniature art gallery. If this option is chosen, a certain amount of restraint is essential. A few light and cheery paintings, tastefully arranged, are always preferable to a large collection plastered on the walls in no apparent order, as if the real intention were to cover the whole surface. A crowded, disorganized effect should be avoided at all costs.

• The hallway will look shorter and wider if the floor covering has transversal stripes or a checkerboard pattern.

• Using the same light color for the walls and furniture will make the hallway look more spacious.

• The lighting should be even and come from the ceiling, but a light coming from near the floor will produce a surprisingly varied effect. Pleasant and original lamps will also add personality to what is usually a drab and colorless area.

• An antique chair or an arrangement of plants at the end of the hallway will be enough to change its appearance.

Before starting to decorate the hallway, look at it for a while and let your imagination run free. Don't be afraid to consider possibilities that might at first glance seem extreme or impractical; you'll be surprised at how much you can do with it. Never underestimate this area; it has unlimited possibilities.

Since the hallway here is not too wide, the best solution was to leave it free of furniture. In order to reduce the distance, a curtain has been put up halfway along the hallway.

One use of a staircase is to delimit various spaces within the same room. Two or three steps are enough to indicate clearly where the kitchen begins and the living room ends.

A good distribution of space must be planned very carefully, because once the work is finished, it is very difficult to rectify any errors. Here, we can see an example of a good distribution of space in which the kitchen and the dining room possess a logical relationship.

A bicycle can brighten up an otherwise dull hallway. The resulting effect is somewhat like a futuristic sculpture decorated with a basket of flowers. The most common examples of this combination of mechanical objects and natural plants are the wheelbarrows used in many gardens as casual supports for flower pots.

In this spartan entrance, a 1950s-style bicycle stands next to some sliding shelves. Alternatives like this one, with its shocking, almost surrealistic effect, can at times be the only way integrate a bicycle into the general decorative scheme of a house.

Decorating the walls

Walls are an integral part of the architectural structure, and the defining element of any space. As such, they are immediately resourceful for their wide range of possible functions; supporting furniture, hanging shelving, backing up bookshelves, attaching lighting and appliances, etc. Their decoration never constitutes a complicated task, and it can be accomplished through various means. It isn't difficult to repaint, or change wallpaper, and the choice depends upon the personal wants and needs of each individual.

Neither is it a problem to plaster or stucco them. Nonetheless, it is vital that the walls are used as a means to support objects, such as paintings, mirrors, ceramics or photographs, all of which serve only as decoration. In this respect, it is important to keep the equilibrium and proportion of the forms in mind, since the symmetry and composition of the shapes are indispensable concepts for adorning walls. And so, for example, if among the collection of items there is some of large size, they should be compensated by another of similar proportion (or a group of smaller items that together make up a collection.) If not, the large item will overwhelm those that are smaller, and a sense of dis-equilibrium will result.

The exposition of a group of pieces of similar size is always decorative. If the objects don't present any formal relationship to each other, colors or textures can be grouped. Many times, a pretty space carefully decorated can appear boring due to the lack of some imaginative decorative details that otherwise offer the needed spark. Here are some ideas to help you overcome this problem:

Framed art. No one doubts that a painting is by its nature highly decorative. But when the time comes to hang it, there are certain norms which should be followed:

• Every painting doesn't belong in every space or on every wall. The theme of the painting, and its chromatic tones, are elements that must be considered when selecting a painting for the home.

• It isn't appropriate to hang small paintings alone on large expanses of wall space.

• A large painting, if standing alone, shouldn't be larger than any furniture that may be below it.

• To put into harmony the overwhelming sensation that a large painting may provoke, a group of paintings should be hung on another wall, or some ornamental object should be placed to the side of the large painting, such as a plant, a lamp or sculpture that acts as a counterpoint.

• Paintings must be hung at eye level of a person either seated of standing. If a group of paintings forms a collection, the height of the central line of the collection should be the guide.

• A painting should never be hung with just one nail.

• On a light-colored wall, a dark-colored frame will always improve the appearance of the painting.

Collection of pieces. There are certain objects (ceramics, small, antique utensils, etc.) which, taken together, can form a group that can constitute a wonderful decorative element. But the arrangement of these objects must also follow some established criteria, as follows:

• The selected objects that together constitute a decorative element must have some nexus, or something in common.

• A collection of objects hung in a vertical line will elevate the visual sensation of the ceiling. By the same reasoning, if a

The appearance of this wall, decorated using the bicolor technique, which is applied with a palette knife, produces a highly pictorial effect.

The combination of the same tones with different painting techniques and drawn motifs lend a provençal look to a small bathroom.

The tromp l´oeil technique applied to walls produces a sensation of depth. And when here, combined with restored and stripped antique furniture, creates a neoclassical atmosphere.

collection is hung horizontally, the room will appear wider.

• Pieces that form a collection, such as illustrations or photographs, must be coherent with the environment in which they are hung as well as with each other.

• It isn't appropriate to hang large items together with smaller ones. It breaks the aesthetic equilibrium and exaggerates the size of the larger.

• The coherence of a collection can be created on the basis of sizes, colors, forms or even the themes of each item.

• The repetition of a theme offers many possibilities and allows one to group together many different sizes, colors and styles. And so, for example, in the space beside a window, a collection of old photographs or posters can be hung that pertain to windows. A group of illustrations can be hung on a wall that will capture the coherence through the harmonious use of the color and material of the frames.

• An asymmetrical arrangement of pictures, if well thought out, can give personality and character to the environment.

A corner devoted to a monographic theme such as flowers combined with paintings, fabrics and vases achieves a personal and romantic atmosphere.

Two in one

Working from the concept of a suite, which brings together a dressing room, bathroom and even bedroom, the bathroom can be conceived as a large room that can be used comfortably and privately by more than one person at a time. This is only possible, of course, in a house that is large enough to arrange the bedroom and bathroom as two interdependent, rather than isolated, rooms.

The first step is to fit out the bathroom so that it can be used comfortably by two people at the same time. To achieve this, some elements will need to be duplicated, while others will have to be made more private than usual. It's not hard to find double washbasins, with everything necessary for two users: two mirrors, lights, basins, faucets, cabinets, etc. Apart from this, you can install two soap dishes, towel racks and stools, so that both people can make use of the room without getting in each other's way.

The main elements (toilet, shower, bathtub) don't need to duplicated, since if one is being used, the other person can use the rest. It is, however, essential to make them as independent as possible: a glass partition or cabin for the toilet, for example can prevent problems of privacy or odors.

The second aspect to be considered in creating a multipurpose bathroom is to distinguish two areas, wet and dry. The wet area contains the toilet, tub and shower, while the dry section contains the washbasin and is used for shaving, putting on makeup, hair styling, manicure and pedicure.

The sections can be separated by a partition and their different personalities can be highlighted by different decorating styles. Other ways to separate is by creating a split-level space with connecting steps or to use different colors on the floor or walls.

Whatever the case, the methods used to differentiate between the two areas should be stylistic or conceptual, or at least using glass, in order to maintain the feeling of space and unity in the room without impeding freedom of movement.

Solid or opaque elements, such as partitions or walls, break up the space and destroy some of the most important characteristics of this type of room: spaciousness and a feeling of unity among the different elements and services.

A dressing room can also be created between the bedroom and bathroom. This could contain all the closets and dressers that would normally be found in the bedroom. Besides gaining space in the bedroom, it can be used for getting dressed early in the morning without bothering anyone.

One final idea would be to include a small gym or fitness center, space and budget permitting. The ever-increasing level of education and information in the modern world has resulted in a growing interest in health and physical fitness. If the bathroom has enough space, it can be the ideal location for fitness equipment such as an exercise bike and weights, or even a Jacuzzi or mini-sauna. The possibilities are endless, and the end result can be stunning.

If you decide to combine a work area with a bedroom within a large space, a correct arrangement of the furniture is paramount and the ornamentation should reflect the personality of its user. Here, a large chest of drawers has been used to divide the room in two.

The lower wall has been painted a different color to differentiate it from the upper part. It is equipped with a stainless steel towel rack with antique fixtures. The marble counter is decorated with large bouquets of mimosa.

A large bedroom can be converted into a suite organized into a space containing both the bedroom area and a bathroom with a shower. The trunk adorned with mimosa provides an excellent division between the two areas. The touch of color adds contrast to the pastel blue walls and the wrought iron headrest.

The inclusion of a small toilet in the master bedroom gives the impression of large and open space. It is a good decorative solution.

The combination of a kitchen and a studio lends a very suggestive Bohemian air as well as being practical since there is access to running water

Even if the bathroom space has to be shared, the ideal solution is to create maximum independence between the two users. The two washbasins here are completely separated. The mirror, placed within a teak frame made out of a bed headrest, unifies the two.

Knocking down walls, removing floors and creating split-level areas is the best way to gain space and capture the maximum amount of light.

In modern decoration false walls and small rooms must be removed. Diaphaneity, light and space are the aspects most sought after and valued in the distribution of a dwelling.

Nonetheless, apartments rarely have the necessary space to provide these requisites, therefore, in order to tear down barriers, it is best to opt for creating rooms that serve more than one function: kitchen-living rooms, bedroom with a bathroom (bathtub and washbasin being left unconcealed, apartments comprising one space, etc.

One of the most interesting options that the market can offer when one is looking for a home, is that of purchasing an old standard apartment which can then be reformed into a comfortable, light and cheerful place to live.

Some apartments even possess the possibility of connecting two floors by means of a staircase and knocking down part of the rooms in order to create a light-filled split-level living space. This solution has all manner of advantages because allows more daylight and makes dwelling a far more pleasant place to live in than its original claustrophobic distribution of tiny rooms.

Most of the examples reproduced here are of modern apartments, which were conceived with a "less is more" idea in mind, that is to say, it is more convenient to have few but very spacious and multi-functional rooms rather than many small and narrow rooms. You can also see on these pages examples of renovations carried out on old apartments. Their distribution has been rectified in order to make the accommodation more consistent with the way we live today. Indeed, if we compare in spa-

tial terms how family life has changed over the last few years with the precious few square meters of urban living space, we can see why the interior structure of dwellings has altered so radically.

For instance, the entrance hall, the independent dinning room, the study... are rooms that have disappeared for the most part, in favor of free, light-filled ones.

Furthermore, the tendency to allow one room to be viewed from another is very much in vogue, first because dwellings are much smaller and second because families are far smaller, therefore there is not such a great need to preserve the intimacy of its dwellers. Another reason for the changes in housing accommodation is the disappearance of domestic service that would often reside in the home they worked. As a result, there is little need to separate rooms.

For example, there is no need to isolate the kitchen from the rest of the house if family meals are simpler, without stews and fried dishes that smell and produce fumes. This, together with technological advances in extractor fans that can keep both the kitchen and the bathrooms odor-free, allows these two spaces to coexist with other rooms.

Therefore spaces must be converted into rooms with a double purpose. Below the mezzanine, which has been turned into a practical bedroom, a small kitchen and an attractive conical basin have been installed. At the end nearest the household appliances, an "island" houses the sink and a useful surface that can be used as a dinning table.

A small living area can be included in a large bedroom, furnishing it with a sofa and some occasional tables. On the other side of the false wall, a washbasin stands out against the gray-ochre tiling that protects the area from splashes of water.

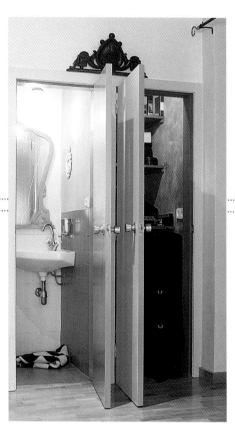

A pair of adjacent doors, both of the same model, give way to two independent areas, but with very distinct decorative solutions. On the left, a washbasin with a mirror that visually augments the space and on the right, an office area for storing all manner of objects of the shelves put up there.

The sliding door in this part of the house opens up to reveal a children´s bedroom with a wooden crib. The space also be doubles as a playroom.

Details, lighting and plants

There is nothing so pleasant as contemplating the final details to add to the decoration. As opposed to the abstractness involved in conceiving a space that is both functional and aesthetic, the detail is more concrete, easier to understand and, in many cases, fascinating. It may be a picture of some kind, a corner you want to use in a creative way, or a decorative complement to place next to your favorite item of furniture.

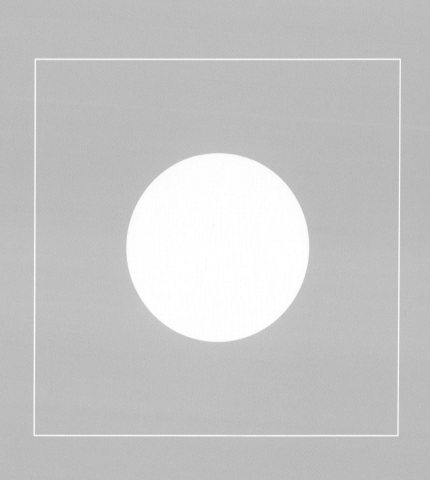

With accent

In art, the artist always desires to focus the spectator's attention to some specific point in a way that is almost unconscious and reflexive. The same thing can be said of a home. Decorative elements must be properly situated to direct the center of attention and control the style, color and characteristics, as well as the disposition of the furniture and other elements that are placed within the confines of a space.

To properly decorate a room, a center of attention should be created by choosing a spot for its visible attraction or by selecting a specific element for its functional importance. Let us take, for example, a dining room table, whose presence and use make it the center of interest in any room, or the aesthetic importance of a chimney to the decoration of a living room.

Properly creating the center of attention by defining spots or placing elements, whether the focus is on essentials like chairs or points of light, or complements such as paintings, decorative elements or auxiliary pieces of furniture, will make the rest of the elements of the room subordinate to them.

≠This will have a profound result on the correct spatial organization of a room. The center of attention permits the room to attain an appropriate aesthetic disposition of the whole, and new subspaces can consequently be created within the larger space, dividing the room into various zones.

This is the significance of an important concept that interior designers call accent. It is the determination of the importance of the elements that form the entirety of the decoration in a room by their strength, function and visual attraction.

The interest in this radical idea resides in using certain elements of a room to establish zones of interest or spots where the eye naturally comes to rest. The room is divided into different spaces without utilizing partitions or dividing furniture. This makes it more functional and flexible. For example, one room can be visually divided into a living room and a dining room by using two elements, a dining room table and a living room table, which become centers of attention around which are placed the rest of the elements. There are various forms for creating accent.

Dominant accent.

This is established when furniture, complements or other elements of a certain size are distributed around a center of interest in such a way that the eye is directed toward it. This is the case of a dining room table surrounded by chairs. Even when the table is the most important element, the accent does not fall solely on it, but on the dining room as a whole.

This sensation of unity can be highlighted with an interplay of contrasting or harmonious colors or by using textures or forms that combine well.

Emphatic accent.

This is attained by giving a special and preeminent attention to a decorative object or architectural element that stands out for its aesthetic beauty. It is appropriate for items like chimneys, staircases or even certain works of art, which by their nature serve as a focal point that lends personality and character to a room.

Although this shouldn't be overemphasized, its presence should be accentuated through the use of some decorative technique, such as through the interplay of accessories that surround and complement it, or by giving it a special color, or by highlighting it via the use of a particular form of illumination.

One wall of a classical living room, adorned with a selection of photographs arranged in apparent disarray, can serve as the center of attraction.

To adorn a table is to arrange the silverware and glass service in an elegant manner. Several delicate blue china bowls have been placed on a damask tablecloth, which lends a fresh and elegant air to the whole.

A discreet, hand-made kilim lends this area a note of elegance while contrasting with the sober lines of the flooring.

Subtle accent.

This consists of creating small and subdued zones that are decorated in a discrete but personal way to establish an intimate ambiance and to balance the decorative whole. They are not centers of interest in themselves, but are indispensable to compensate for the excessive visual strength of some areas of the room or for the coldness of others (for example, the area for the telephone stand in a living room or the nightstands in a bedroom).

Subordinate accent.

This is the effect that a room's structure, the ceiling, the walls and the floor, creates. Normally, the way in which these parts of a room are treated depend on the dimensions of the room, its function and the elements that are included within it. They must take on a subordinate role since they occupy a large part of the overall decorative whole of the space, and if these parts are too dominating, the room will appear heavy and overbearing.

The small living room is very exotic

Coming in on the right foot

In today's world, the square footage available in a dwelling is a luxury. More often than not, it´s subject to constant restrictions. For this reason, more than any other, the entrance hall, with the grandiose first impression it intended to make in previous epochs, has become a thing of the past.

In small homes, the tendency has been to eliminate it altogether, using the space to augment vital living areas.

Nonetheless, the entrance hall remains important, since it gives a visitor the all-important first impression, and, in many ways, defines the rest of the house. It also reflects the personalities of those who live there. And so, even though it involves a small space, the entrance hall is an ancillary area that in many ways should not be overlooked.

At first, it wouldn't seem excessively difficult to decorate the hallway to a house. Since we are dealing with a small or medium-sized space at most, it would be inappropriate to overload the room with furniture and other objects.

Still, the reception area, although its dimensions are reduced, must have its own style and at the same time be a true anteroom to the rest of the dwelling. In this respect, there are some general guidelines that should be kept in mind.

• It is important to distinguish the entrance from the rest of the façade to avoid any stark contrasts. Whether the entrance is entered directly from the street, from a small elevator, or from a dark hallway, it is a good idea to create a cheerful and welcoming environment, using, for example, plants, some framed pictures, imaginative lighting or walls painted in warm tones.

• No matter how small the space, all reception areas permit the inclusion of something that gives it character. A small bookshelf and a clothes rack, or a simple decorative detail can be sufficient to create the desired atmosphere.

• If space is not a limiting factor, there are various things to consider when decorating the entrance. It might be helpful to include a piece of furniture, such as a small chest, preferably with some drawers, so that in addition to having some flat surfaces for putting decorative objects on, there is a place to keep letters, invoices, keys, pencils or even telephone books. Other items that should be considered include a closet for coats, or, if one isn't available, a clothes rack; an umbrella stand that could also hold a decorative walking stick or cane; and last but not least, a mirror, which offers a nice decorative touch and serves to make this smaller-sized room appear larger. A mirror is also quite useful for that last glance before leaving the house.

• Entrances must feel warm and inviting, and so lighting is quite important. It must be kept in mind that the lighting must not dazzle, but at the same time a home's entrance must not be cloaked in semi-darkness. This, more than anything else, out of consideration for visitors. If natural light is not available, a low-voltage lamp is the most practical solution, along with some spotlights directed toward the ceiling or floor, or toward some specific spot on a shelf. Keep in mind the importance of assuring that the light switches and doorbells are in plain view, accessible and easy to use.

• Because we are dealing with one of the most frequently used spaces in the house due to all of the comings and goings, and since the reception room is often used additionally as a place to store objects, the floor must be strong. It also goes without saying that the floor shouldn't be made of slippery-surfaced material.

A coat of a pumpkin-colored paint to emphasize the star, a simple wooden bench and a rug are the elements chosen to organize this small entrance.

A translucent sculpture, which contrasts copper with the delicateness of cherry blossom, lends the room an ethereal effect.

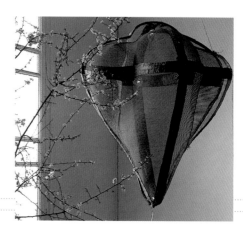

The hallway and corridor have also been very sympathetically restored

• If the original architectural structure of the house does not include a reception room, there are usually options, such as placing an armoire facing the entrance, which will create the appearance of a division in a space that will nonetheless allow free passage into the house. Another possibility is to place shelving, such as a two-faced bookshelf. One face can serve as a library for the living room while the other side, facing the door, will provide room to put some small piece of auxiliary furniture on.

It should be noted once again that although dwellings at times don't offer many options, or at least make the possibility of various solutions difficult, imagination, a bit of taste, and some time well-spent when planning the decoration can go a long way to discovering new ideas and interesting combinations.

A minimalist flat surface painted gray provides space to leave things. A touch of color is added by a pop art painting.

Working in comfort

One of the difficulties with interior design is that it must unite two concerns that in principal seem contradictory: privacy and social interaction. On the one hand, everyone needs private space, isolated from the noise and bustle that others generate. On the other hand, every house should anticipate a certain level of hospitality and should be properly prepared to welcome friends and allow for the possibility of social engagements or get-togethers. This matter is accentuated when a member of the household works at home.

Times have long since past when certain professions, such as doctors, architects and lawyers, had their offices and studies in their own home, which, by the way, were much larger than is common today. Nevertheless, given the current economic situation and the changes in the workplace, every day more and more people are either deciding or are forced by necessity to work at own home. Individuals such as small artisans, independent businessmen, and professionals such as publicists, graphic designers and journalists, have found that working at home is more convenient.

If possible, logic dictates that a specific room be dedicated solely for work, so that the room can be furnished with furniture and other items that are most convenient for the job, without being concerned with the general aesthetics of the rest of the home. If, for example, a small workshop is desired, such as an art studio or carpentry shop, the specific furniture and tools of the trade may be used, along with an especially resistant floor, appropriate ventilation, and adequate sound-proofing, so as to avoid interference with the rest of the house. The space could also be converted into an office incorporating the chairs, tables, and shelving an other office furniture, deriving the comfort, concentration and atmosphere appropriate for working.

In any case, given that the issue is one of creating the right working environment, the choice of furniture, as well as the design of the layout, must be planned for optimum practicality, always keeping in mind the purpose for which the space is to be used. A journalist or writer cannot work in a space without a library or places to save magazines, various papers and the general information that constitute the materials used for daily consultation. A jeweler who decides to put his workshop in his house will need at his disposal a number of drawers and shelves to properly store and classify the distinctive tools, jewels and minerals of his trade. An independent small businessman will make his work easier if he has file cabinets within arm's reach, a comfortable chair with wheels and high back, a large work table that includes a telephone, and other auxiliary chairs to receive visitors.

In any case, there will never be enough shelves, drawers, pencil holders and other work items, even though it would seem so when first setting up. If everything that pertains to the decoration of a work area is dedicated to placing the work space in order, then it is an absolute maxim that the work environment and everything associated with it, including the distribution of the materials, is never too much.

In all areas destined to be developed for professional activities, which is understood to be a daily dedication, an aspect to which special attention must be paid is the lighting, indispensable for the working environment. If there is a window in the room, the table must be placed as near as feasibly possible to it, and never with its back to it, so as to take advantage of the daylight hours.

Artificial illumination must consist of a generalized central point of light with one or more table lamps. All types of lamps

A work area needs enough light. Two powerful lamps illuminate the area, highlighting the wooden sculptures.

The area below the mezzanine is used as an area for working with the computer. The staircase also doubles as shelving where books and papers can be stored. Next to it, a table serves as a reading area.

The work area must always be kept tidy. The tools and accessories must be arranged properly so that are always at hand. Small cans have been used here to keep brushes in and, in the foreground, several bowls are used for mixing colors. At the back, some shelves hold books and all manner of objects.

are commercially available, from flexible head lamps to halogen spotlights, all of which come in a wide variety of models and sizes, and which can be adapted to a wide range of functions. Usually it may entail nothing more than installing a small spotlight from the ceiling or attached to a wall that directs the light to a specific point, such as shelves or a library that is frequently used.

If there is enough space, one might consider including more than one table, one for each particular task. For example, the telephone could be placed on a small table, while a larger table is to be used for books, magazines and documents. A round table may also be included, surrounded by chairs, for small meetings. Since tables occupy quite a bit of space, they should be placed against the length of the walls.

When the time comes to elect the proper type of furniture, one will be faced with various options. Custom-made furniture, designed specifically for the space, comes with the advantage that the drawers and shelving can be designed to personal taste.

A light space painted with a stucco decoration that filters light, thanks to the curtains, provides various work areas. A large table with a computer on it, an area for watching television and a corner next to the wall used to store files and other items.

The longest wall in this room has been used to install a work station and a shelf for holding all manner of objects. In order to make the area blend in with the rest of the room, it has been painted white, which contrasts with the old tiled floor and the moldings on the ceiling.

The obvious drawback to this option is the higher cost involved.

Another option is to acquire prefabricated furniture (bookshelves, file cabinets and drawers,) and fitting them into the available space. If space is at a premium, the best solution is to purchase modules that are adaptable and can be adjusted to fit the needs.

Finally, in order to ensure efficient use of a work area in the home, one must´t forget those small details that are so necessary to an office; paper, pen and pencil holders, plastic or cork bulletin boards to attach notes or papers. If possible, one shouldn't forget the decorative details, (paintings, ceramics, etc.) and more than anything, plants. As small and unassuming as they are, plants lend a touch of cheerfulness to any room, brightening what might otherwise be a cold, sterile environment.

The truth is that most homes suffer from such space limitations that dedicating a room solely for work is impossible, and so the work area must be included in a room already in use. When this is the case, some things have to be taken into account.

Objects must be placed on shelves in a logical order and in groups. A simple white wooden surface is ideal for keeping books and other objects on. The area below the shelf has been taken advantage to hand a few pictures.

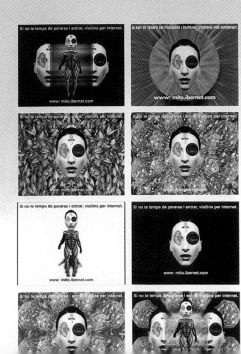

A small room for a study

Although in some ways life has become notably more difficult, it is also true that a generally higher economic level, more information, a cultural restlessness, a desire to learn or practice new activities have gradually created new needs that require new areas in the home.

Many people today feel the need for a place in some small, quiet corner of the house where they get away from the noise and distractions of life and study, read, write or carry out some activity, be it painting, model building, working, fashion design or whatever.

It is also true that each day more and more people are finding reasons to work at home, due in part to the increase in service professions that before were less prevalent, such as translators, computer programmers, accountants, etc., as well as new conditions and necessities that modern lifestyles and labor characteristics are imposing. Everyday there are more and more freelance jobs. And so, because of these factors, it is becoming important to set aside a work area or study when planning and distributing the space of a home.

During the end of the 1970's it began to be almost normal to install a work place at home. At this time it was discovered that a study was equally valid as much for administrators, small independent businesses, or sales representatives and insurance agents as it was for journalists, artists or writers. Today it isn't unusual to find individuals working at home for a second income to supplement the primary income, or others who dedicate a good number of hours that their normal work offers them to develop certain hobbies like learning a new language, writing, surfing the internet, or simply reading, and who need their own quiet space for concentration.

If work is carried out all day at home, or if the house is sufficiently large, the best option is to set aside an entire room as a study. This is worth doing, even if it means reorganizing the living space by, for example, moving wardrobes and other items in a walk-in closet if one large enough exists, or even sacrificing a living room. Anything is appropriate if it creates a comfortable study. There one can receive visitors such as clients or colleagues in a professional environment. If the office space were surrounded by unmade beds or simply integrated into the inevitable bustle of domestic life as carried out by the rest of the family, it would damage the professional image.

Nevertheless, the majority of homes lack rooms, and to use an entire room as a study in the type of buildings that exist today, where space is always at a premium, is a luxury that many simply can't afford. So, when the time comes to set aside a corner to study or read, the best solution might be a room that will serve a double function. It is possible that many hours will be spent in the study area, and so the corner must be chosen with care, keeping some basic considerations in mind that will serve to take the maximum advantage of the space and to best facilitate the work or activity that will be realized there. Work is that much more difficult when it is performed under ill-suited conditions.

To assure that the creation of a work area is fruitful, we have some suggested the following advice:

• In the study area, only the most essential elements should be installed.

• Assure that the selected area is quiet, separate from the parts of the house where the other inhabitants normally reside, especially if there are various family members that include chil-

These two practical tables on wheels has been placed near the large window in order to take maximum advantage of the light. Placed against the wall, The movable shelves are very handy to use as storage space.

The work area must always be kept tidy. The tools and accessories must be arranged properly so that are always at hand. Small cans have been used here to keep brushes in and, in the foreground, several bowls are used for mixing colors. At the back, some shelves hold books and all manner of objects.

A restored, old chest of drawers serves as a decorative storage space. The metallic handles increase the amount of light in the room. The top of chest has been used to place several objects in a disordered but harmonious arrangement completes a decoration presided by a period fan.

dren or babies. This will encourage concentration and a relaxed working environment, and avoid the chaos of children running around underfoot.

• Keeping in mind the scarcity of space in modern homes, elect a type of decoration and some furniture that favor the sensation of size and avoid items that would create a hodgepodge style or a feeling of claustrophobia.

• It is appropriate that the selected space be well-lit, having some strong natural lighting where the desk can be near.

• It might be a good idea to paint the walls with soft colors that combine well with the rest of the environment since this will heighten concentration.

• If the auxiliary furniture is also painted with the appropriate colors they can also help to impart a freshness to the study or small office.

As has already been mentioned, the best option for creating a proper work area when there is limited space in the house is to install it in a room that is already serving another function.

The large window illuminates this tiny space that has been turned into a work area where a table and several shelves have been put up. The chair upholstered with fabric, together with the painting, lend the space a discrete elegance.a

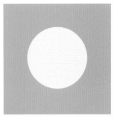

The advantages of high ceilings

In this section, we will present a number of examples of how to take advantage of the space in which we live, not only in a two-dimensional plane, but also in the height of the interior. It all boils down to obtaining the most possible space from the volume as much as the square footage. Undoubtedly, it is a concept that is adapted more for living spaces that have high ceilings, such as apartments in older buildings, but as will be seen, some of the practical possibilities noted here perfectly pertain to all types of homes.

There are two factors that help us make these types of reforms. First, to attempt to take the maximum advantage of the available space in the dwelling. As we all know, space constraints represent a real headache for most families, who are always seeking places for storage, even by attempting to build out new space. Second, to try to establish a different aesthetic form, since ceilings that are too high can lead to a cold and sterile living room, or make a hallway seem narrower than it really is.

If the height so permits, the most radical and most spectacular measure, although it is also the most costly, is to construct a new floor or attic, creating one or more rooms. This new floor would be most appropriate for a bedroom, study, office or a combination of these rooms, since the area would be separate from the rest of the house and so offer the peace that is desired for these types of areas. It should also be mentioned that installing in an upper floor a kitchen or dining room, or even a bathroom is problematical. It is simply too inconvenient to serve meals or clear the table afterward.

The most economical form to create a passage up to the new floor is to install a stair and metallic structure next to one of the walls of the lower room, but there are many other possibilities from which to choose, including spiral staircases.

In dwellings where the ceiling is not sufficiently high to add an entire separate level, installing attic space dedicated for storage may be considered to stow those items or clothes that are not in constant use. This may be constructed in some place in the house that is not a principal room, or along a hallway, by installing a false ceiling between which and the original ceiling suitcases and other items can be stored.

In the children's bedroom there is never enough free space. This is where they play, study, sleep and dress. And so it might be practical to place an elevated platform upon which to place a bed. Below it another bed could be placed if two children sleep in the room. If not, a desk or bookshelf can be installed there, instead.

In the kitchen the most suitable is to construct some wooden shelving high up on the walls that serve to augment the available storage space, or hang from the ceiling various utensils and decorative objects so as to lessen the sense that the ceiling is so high.

Finally, if the only interest is to eliminate the visual sensation of coldness that high ceilings produce, there is always the remedy of installing a false ceiling, or painting the high ceiling in a color that is darker than the color on the walls, since strong colors produce a sensation of proximity and coziness.

A completely bare room, accentuated with a small glass panel that lets in light, demonstrates the aesthetics of white walls, which, in other rooms might reduce space, here visually increases the size thanks to the effect of the light.

This modern design attempts to visually lower the ceiling with a false wall that has been tiled and highlighted with a frame. The dark colors of the window frame produces a desirable contrast with the predominant white.

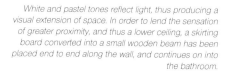

White and pastel tones reflect light, thus producing a visual extension of space. In order to lend the sensation of greater proximity, and thus a lower ceiling, a skirting board converted into a small wooden beam has been placed end to end along the wall, and continues on into the bathroom.

Another way of creating the sensation of lower ceilings is by painting them in a warm tone and fitting imbedded spotlights directed toward specific points. Hinged doors have not been installed between the dining room and the living room in order to make the atmosphere airy. In addition, a sliding glass door takes up one side of the room, which heightens further still the sensation of continuity and spaciousness.

Controlling natural light

If there is a characteristic that must be placed before all others when the time comes to select a future home, it is undoubtedly daylight. An attractive and well-decorated apartment that lacks natural light simply cannot overcome a sense of sadness and squalor. On the other hand, a home that is humbly furnished, if it enjoys enough daylight, is sure to transmit optimism and cheer.

In all homes the sun is what provides natural lighting. It enters the house through various openings: normal windows, glass doors, skylights, and even glassed walls.

The ideal situation is when daylight enters all of the rooms in the house in sufficient amounts so that during daytime hours no supplementary electrical lighting is necessary. This type of illumination, aside from saving energy and lowering electricity bills, gives a room a much more natural, cheerful and lively appearance than one lit with artificial lighting. Interior designers or the inhabitants themselves do not have much say in the matter of natural light. It remains in the hands of the architects. Nevertheless, when the time comes to choose a home, it is interesting to keep the theme of lighting in mind, since sunlight markedly influences the decoration of an environment. The intensity of sunlight will affect the aesthetics of tones and textures. It is preferable to opt for an apartment that might be less attractive but which is brighter and lets in more sun over one that is possibly better distributed but dark and lacking natural light.

The desire to control sunlight and adapt it to the needs and preferences of its inhabitants of a home has forced decorators to expend a lot of effort in developing various options in response to a type of illumination that is ever-changing in intensity and orientation, depending on the hour of the day and the time of the year.

Every aperture in a house offers many possibilities for controlling the amount of daylight entering without forgetting the ornamental effects that it can lend to the overall space. Let us take one example. When a normal wooden door is open, it allows in not only people, but also wind, rain and light. When it is closed, it becomes another element of the house, and the way it fits into the decorative whole will be a function of its form, material, color and finishing touches. Nevertheless, if in its place a glass door is installed, when closed it will still allow all of the outside light to enter, unquestionably lending a distinct aesthetic aspect to the indoor environment. Reflections and sunlight continue to enter, and the colors and textures inside absorb the light, while the strength and naturalness of the light itself becomes part of the decorative interplay.

Depending on the space where the aperture is found, its treatment varies: security bars, glass doors, all types of blinds, lace curtains or drapes.

Curtains carry out an important function. They protect the intimacy of the inhabitants, expand or reduce the perceived space and regulate the daylight that can at times be bothersome and cause unwanted reflections. But at the same time they are quite decorative. They adorn windows and add a touch of color, life, warmth and personality to a room.

Every environment in a house will require a different treatment. In living rooms or dining rooms where more natural light generally enters, curtains of a certain thickness are appropriate so that while watching television, for example, bothersome glares can be completely avoided. For children's bedrooms perhaps more translucent curtains are appropriate which, when closed, still allow a good amount of light to enter. This room is often used in the afternoons, when sunlight is not so strong,

Rooms with normal-size windows, or that face north or connect to a light well should be covered with a simple white screen, which prevents undesirable views to been seen and protects the intimacy of the occupant, while allowing the maximum amount of light through.

Lace curtains must be gathered to look elegant within the general decorative scheme. In reality, they should always be three times as wide as the window. Vertical lines look svelte and light.

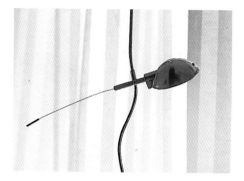

Nowadays, there are many textile manufacturers that design a wide range of curtains for filtering light and that can be adapted to numerous decorative styles and possibilities. It is important to hang curtains that filter light without blocking out the exterior view of a garden or a landscape.

and with this type of fabric two objectives are attained; maintaining privacy while allowing in a good amount of sunlight.

Lace curtains are quite appropriate for both bathrooms and kitchens because of their transparency, since these rooms frequently allow much less natural light to enter than in other areas of the house.

One good idea, quite fashionable today, is to combine window curtains with Venetian blinds. In this way, when maximum sunlight is desired, the curtains can be opened completely while the blinds will assure that no one is looking in. In the mid-afternoon, the curtains can be drawn a bit, which will immediately lend a new aspect to the room. It is helpful to keep in mind here that lighter tones create an effect of greater space, while darker tones, though not recommended for small rooms, lend a space a sense of seclusion.

Blinds, shutters and awnings are very useful for regulating the amount of entering light and heat, and for maintaining privacy. Of course, they are more simple and less ornamental than curtains, but on the other hand, they are immensely practical.

Thanks to the glass doors, the skylight and the lattice door, the breadth and transparency of this hallway is enhanced. Abundant space is somewhat of a luxury nowadays. On the few occasions when it is possible to use space as decoration, it is worth doing, since the result is exceptionally attractive.

Indoor lighting

Each area of the house requires a different type of illumination. The choice of lighting will depend on aesthetic and functional criteria. If you are able control the lighting in your home, you will be able to manipulate the rooms according to your own taste.

Three types of lights, which work in conjunction, are needed to illuminate a room. A standing lamp provides the ambiental lighting and aids movement about the room. Two lamps focussed on specific surfaces of the living room, such as for reading or sewing, etc, also help to lend a room a feeling of coziness.

Entrances and hallways are frequently transited areas where no specific activity is carried out. Therefore they only need to be illuminated with indirect lighting. The most appropriate are spotlights and wall lamps, because they do not take up space and, consequently, do not obstruct movement. Large lamps and table lamps should be avoided for this area of the dwelling.

Regarding the bedroom, there are three points to keep in mind: you should be able to turn the lights on and off from the bed; the light used to read must be suitable; and the ambiental lighting must be relaxing. Light switches will have to be installed next to the headrest and next to the door, and they should control all the bedroom lighting. With respect to the best type of ambiental illumination, the light should have a shade and the bulb should be of the incandescent variety. The reading lamp must be strong, directional and have a folding arm.

The kitchen is the room that requires more illumination than any other room. Since a variety of activities are carried out here: eating, working, reading, ironing, etc. So the lighting must be placed high up, be it on the ceiling lights or a fluorescent tube (which has the advantage that it is a low-consumption form of illumination and produces much light).

The work surfaces will also have to be illuminated, the best solution being to install spotlights below the highest cupboards. If this is not possible in your kitchen, the next best solution is to install direction spotlights on the ceiling or on the walls (about 1.70 m above the floor). If the kitchen has an eating area, a ceiling lamp should be hung over the middle of the table; if possible, the best choice would be the kind that can be raised and lowered.

The illumination of the dining room must always be centered. The best advice is to hang a lamp from the ceiling above the center of the dining table. It should be suspended about 90 cm above the surface of the table. The installation of a dimmer allows you to adjust the intensity of the light in order to create the right mood for each occasion.

With respect to the study or office, it is essential to keep in mind that your health and capacity of concentration are at stake. Therefore a good reading light is required. The light in question should be adjustable with a concentrated and direct beam. It should be placed to the left of the user so as not to cast shadows when writing.

In order to prevent glare, the bulb must be masked by a shade and should be positioned at the height of the eyes. Incandescent bulbs are the most recommendable, as they are warm and relaxing, or the halogen type, which do not confuse colors.

In order to illuminate the areas of this kitchen, the best solution is to install a row of spotlights suspended from the ceiling that illuminate only the most essential areas, thus avoiding unnecessary glare.

In order to highlight this elegant corner, a rococo console has been placed there on top of which a table lamp sits whose light is cast over a coffee set, producing an interplay between the different volumes of the cups.

If you do not have much space, the dinning room table should be transparent in order to lend the sensation of space.

A bedroom can be filled with flowers with the help of a Nordic quilt which acts as a counterbalance to the sober decoration.

Like a garden

Sadly enough, it seems that every day there are fewer green areas in cities. Nonetheless, people need to feel they are in contact with nature, especially given the frenetic lifestyles in today's world. This is amply demonstrated not only in the custom of escaping to the country for the weekends, but also with the fact that it is rare not to find a house with some type of plant or flower among its decorative elements.

This shouldn't be surprising, given that vegetation significantly enriches the aspect and atmosphere of any room. Rare is the home that doesn't benefit from some greenery, or the decorative object that doesn't seem more attractive when accompanied by a well-cared-for plant.

When the time comes for choosing a plant, you should make sure the lighting is appropriate for the plant selected, as much as deciding what size, shape and variety is desired. Large plants, logically, visually reduce the space, while small plants never seem adequate in large areas.

The largest indoor plants can be used to divide a space into two, or to delimit two distinct environments, for example, between a living and dining area, to make the relaxing or reading areas more restful and comfortable.

Large indoor plants can also serve as a counterpoint to large elements within a space (on either side of a door or window, near a bookcase, or to balance the presence of a large painting). They are also appropriate for occupying those dead areas that every house possesses; narrow hallways, small entrances, an alcove below the stairs, or even a chimney, if left unused.

Small plants have the same possibilities as any other ornamental object, and can be exhibited individually on shelves, furniture, tables, window sills, or even hung in a basket suspended from the ceiling. A shelf attached to a wall is ideal for hanging plants such as ivy. Just let it grow. If the desired plant is of the flowering variety, its coloring, form and texture should obviously be chosen to complement the other decorative elements.

Another recommendable option is to group together different types of small plants and flowers.

Interior plants greatly complement the decorative aspect of a bedroom, affording freshness and charm, and with an available window they are no great expense. In fact, because of their relative inexpensiveness, when you are just beginning to decorate your home, your plants can be used to fill up the free spaces, substituting them later for the desired elements as they are discovered. An abundance of plants is very much recommended for a large space with a lot of natural light and indirect artificial light.

Light is essential for plants, and their placement must depend upon the amount of light available and the particular needs of the species. If there is not a sufficient amount of natural light available in the house, artificial light may be used, which, when used properly, will render even better results.

As in other decorative elements, a few plants carefully selected and properly displayed will create a much better result than an invasion of plants in a room or a shelf, which can produce an effect contrary to the intention.

The design of these lamps and the combination of furniture from different areas of the world provide an eclectic atmosphere.

The trompe l´oeil in the large photograph imitating a vegetable motif brings to life an otherwise dull ceiling. Another trompe l´oeil painted on canvas and upholstered in the English style, depicting a classical landscape, lends a touch of elegance. In the small photograph, sitting on the window ledge, a small bouquet of flowers contrasts with the elegant oldness of the paint.

A small terrace on the ground floor has undergone a transformation thanks to the trompe l´oeil that simulates a garden wall with an arch. This visual trick has been further enhanced by installing a low wooden platform on which a parasol stands.

In order to protect plants from direct sunlight, various blinds that filter the light have been situated. The highly original vegetable fiber lamps give this area of the balcony a very intimate air.

The room reproduced in this volume belong to the following interior decorators and other professionals:

Adela cabré (Diagonal Verd), Interiorismo / Berta lozano, interiorista / Betty Miller (Demy Lune), Interiorismo / Carmen Balada, ceramista; Manuel Arenas, arquitecto, pintor / Carmen Murtra, interiorista; Pedro mayans, interiorista, anticuario (Hotel San Ignasi) / Cesc sola, interiorista / Cesc Sola, Ana Pla, interioristas /Claudia Valcells, interiorista, Pinturas Especiales / Clementina Lizcano, interiorista, Montajes Efímeros / Cristina Rodríguez, interiorista / Elisabeth Sabala, pintora / Francesca Saludes, Andreas Lewe / Ignacio Arbeola, Montse Boley, Silvia Ortega, arquitectos / Ima Sanchis Jost, escritora, periodista / Ines Rodriguez, arquitecto / Irene Jorda, Bau Art Partner Gremmels Pacher, Arquitectura, Interiorismo / Julia Ensesa, decoradora / Julia Ensesa, Santy Prats, Natalia Gomez, decoradora, arquitecto, Proyecto Color / Lala Rubio, restauración / Maite Cornet, decoradora, atrezzo / Marc jesús, pintor, escultor / María Torrontegui, Trampantojos, Pintura Decorativa /Metro estudi, Jose Mª Casaponsa, Lourdes Alba, interioristas / Mireya de Sierra, Jose Mª Tort / Natalia Ferrer, Ivo presas, traductora, músico / Natalia Gomez Angelats, interiorista, Proyectos Color / Natalia Gomez Angelats, Javier Navarro, interioristas / Nuria Ribó, periodista / Pata Garbó, Jordi Carbonell, Medicina /Pepa Poch, Pinturas Decorativas, Interiorismo, Estilismo, P. Tejidos /Per Domus, Gemma Peiro, Arquitectura, Interiorismo / Raquel Cohen, Escultura / RemediosBenavent, Dani Boix, Restauración / Reyes Ventos, Montajes Efímeros / Rodrigo Prats, arquitecto / Rogelio Jimenez, Patricia Antón, Arquitectura, Traducciones / Rossi Innes / Ruben Gomez, Escultor / Silvia Barnils, Jaume Cardellach, Cerámica, Restauración / Teó Henning, Franc Miller, diseñadores, Pinturas Especiales .